A Miraculous Life

DIANNE SHOBER

WESTBOW
PRESS®
A DIVISION OF THOMAS NELSON
& ZONDERVAN

WestBow Press books may be ordered through booksellers or by contacting:

WestBow Press
A Division of Thomas Nelson & Zondervan
1663 Liberty Drive
Bloomington, IN 47403
www.westbowpress.com
1 (866) 928-1240

Interior Image Credit: Brusheezy.com

ISBN: 978-1-9736-6373-7 (sc)
ISBN: 978-1-9736-6375-1 (hc)
ISBN: 978-1-9736-6374-4 (e)

Library of Congress Control Number: 2019906220

Print information available on the last page.

WestBow Press rev. date: 06/11/2019

Introduction

Miracles. Those wondrous moments of the inexplicable, when amazing things happen that can only be orchestrated by the hand of God. Through these brief vignettes easily accessible in morning or evening devotions, this book explores the many events in Scripture when God intervenes in the lives of ordinary people and creates extraordinary outcomes. Beginning in the New Testament with the numerous incidents when Jesus and later His disciples seek transformation in the human body, mind and spirit, we learn how He made the impossible possible. But just as importantly, we see how God intends for us to believe and experience the same miracles for our lives. This is what makes the living Word active in our lives – when Scripture comes to life for us and triggers change in us, an explosion of faith that exclaims: "Our God is able."

The text not only delves into New Testament episodes, but also works its way through amazing Old Testament events which describe God moving across the earth and in the lives of people to reform nothingness into magnificence, heartache into joy, tragedy into triumph. After all, isn't that what the Holy Spirit seeks to do in us every single day of our lives?

I hope you enjoy this book and its re-imagining of the miraculous in the Bible. It was birthed through a love for God's Word, shared on Christian radio and seasoned through life experiences. May each story affect a meaningful impact in your walk with Jesus.

"You have seen the Lord perform all these mighty deeds with your own eyes." Deuteronomy 11:7

Dianne Shober
March 27, 2019

Contents

The Miracles of Life

As a new year approaches, very often each of us search for a word from the Lord that will set the tone of the year. The one word that I have been praying for, anticipating, looking to see, is MIRACLES. Any one of us at any given time is asking God to do the impossible – to arrange events, situations, relationships or finances that, when accomplished, illustrate our heavenly Father's divine intervention.

A miracle can be described as an extraordinary or supernatural phenomenon that defies natural or scientific laws and suggests divine agency. It may also be a remarkable event or development that brings very welcome consequences. It can even stand for an outstanding example or achievement. It's interesting to note that these definitions point directly to the finger of God and such events as the resurrection or water to wine indicate His handiwork.

Our relationship with Him, solidified in the verse in Hebrews 11:1 which states that *"Faith is the confidence that what we hope for will actually happen; it gives us assurance about things we cannot see"* suggests that we may not always see what God is doing in our lives, but may still trust His heart. It's important to our spiritual wellbeing to acknowledge and anticipate His intervention in our impossible situations as the rest of the chapter in Hebrews 11 recounts. Does our heart not thrill when we hear of the amazing things that God is doing? Do we not dance and leap like the healed paralytic described in Acts 3?

Yet God is doing such marvellous things every single day and it takes adjusting our senses to life's situations to comprehend His constant engagement in our lives. What miracle are you praying for this year or what miracle are you rejoicing over that has already occurred? Let me recount a few for you that I have recently learned about. My son and his wife have only been married a short time and like many young couples need financial miracles. Their area of Missouri endured a flash flood that buried some roadways in water. Unbeknownst to Jacob and Samantha they thought they could drive their car through a low-lying area and the water would only reach their hub caps. Unfortunately, that wasn't the case; the water reached their engine, flooded it and then water began seeping into the car. Not only was it a frightening situation, but their newly purchased car was ruined.

Unable to purchase another vehicle right away and lacking insurance that covered this "Act of God", they had to depend on others to drive them about as their rural subdivision had no bus transportation available. What was their constant prayer? "God help us get another car." And their church family joined them in this petition. After a few months of being car-less and dependent, a miracle happened. A young couple had been given a car from their grandmother and, as they already had two, didn't need this third vehicle. They offered it to Jacob and Samantha for the amazing sum of $1,00. Yes, that's right – only $1.00. It's a fantastic car with minimal mileage, and in great condition; in fact, it's much better than their previous one. Not only that, a neighbour who is a mechanic, has purchased their ruined car with the intent of fixing it up and selling it. Are they dancing and leaping? You bet they are!

How does this affect me? Well, not only am I delighted to see God reveal Himself in such a loving way to my son and daughter-in-law, and so completely and absolutely answer all of our prayers, but this also gives me encouragement to pray for a vehicle as well and to pray for others who may also need personal transport. When others receive miracles, it helps us believe in them, too. God uses every miracle to extend the level of faith of all His children.

What other things has God done for someone? I returned to the office recently having gone abroad for university business. Chatting with a co-worker I asked how the holidays had been for her. She told me her story of miracles. Her young son was given a scholarship to attend a school and she'd thought it would commence from Grade 8. To her dismay upon reading the school's letter of acceptance, she learned that the scholarship only commenced from Grade 11. As she hadn't applied to any other school, she was desperate to find a school for her son. Her anxiety level went through the roof, compounded by the worried voice of her son who was concerned he didn't have a place to commence his high school studies. Desperately she prayed and searched for a school. Then she found one and following the application and interview process, learned that her son was accepted. She rejoiced! In fact, it was a Christian school which made her even more grateful. Then she realised God's miracles weren't finished. Although she had a place for her son to study, she needed the finances to pay the tuition. "God help again", she cried. Did He? Of course; she received a letter granting him a bursary which reduced the tuition substantially. She wept after receiving all this great news.

Another story of miracles begins many years ago when a young California surfer and a young woman from rural Canada were serving God in their communities, thousands of miles apart. Both had separately heard God say that they'd eventually use their home as a refuge, a place where people could come to be refreshed, encouraged and learn more about God. By a series of supernatural events, they ended up attending the same mega church in the huge city of Los Angeles, but more significantly they began attending the same home group.

With Christmas just around the corner, they threw themselves into ministry and watched one another with quiet admiration. Always eager to share their daily meditations with one another, the young lady spoke out her verse from Isaiah 54:2: *"Enlarge your house, build an addition. Spread out your home and spare no expense."* With a sparkle in his eye, the young man said: "Let me tell you what I believe this verse means" and proceeded to explain his vision for a house of ministry and the remarkable dreams he'd been having of this young lady in this house with his children. After one official date, he asked her to marry him and then they watched as the miracles multiplied.

Having minimal resources to start a new life together, they prayed over every aspect of their wedding, from invitations, to flowers, to rings and caterers and witnessed the countless ways the Lord provided. From the scripture verse they placed on their invitations: 1 John 4:19 *"We love each other because He first loved us,"* which would reference their wedding date April (month 4) 19 as well as the groom's first name, to the vision God gave the groom for his wedding ring of three strands of intertwined gold representing Ecclesiastes 4:12 that *"a triple braided cord is not easily broken"*, they watched in amazement as God set His seal on their union. Thus, three children and thirty-three years of marriage later they have found that God continues to do miracles, and still marvel at the miracles God performs to bring His children together.

This last story brings me to the first miracle that Jesus performed in the New Testament, the wedding miracle of water to wine found in John 2. Jesus was at a wedding: a community celebration that in many cases could last up to seven days. It was a time of great feasting in which everyone enjoyed the generosity of their host. In this instance, the wedding celebration was into its third day with many more to follow when a huge debacle occurred. Perhaps the family hadn't expected so many guests or expected them to be so thirsty or simply lacked additional resources. Whatever the case, they ran out of wine. Can you imagine a celebration in which some people didn't get enough refreshments? It'd be a humiliation to the family and the talk of their neglect would circulate throughout the entire community. What a grave embarrassment.

Perhaps Mary, Jesus mother, was thinking of this when she approached her son and shared the problem. Clearly, she knew who to come to for help. Maybe she'd already seen what He could do; certainly, she knew that Jesus could, as the Son of God, do the impossible [Luke 1:37]. In turn, Jesus knew why He was on earth – to teach the Father's love and to offer His life for the salvation and redemption of souls. Yet He also knew of His ministry to heal the sick, blind, and lame. But a wedding feast? Providing wine? He insisted that this wasn't yet His time or place, but His seemingly abrupt response didn't upset His mother. She trusted her son to do what was best for the situation and instructed the caterers to obey His commands.

Then, assured of the Father's will, Jesus ordered the servants to bring six large thirty gallon jars and fill them with water. Water - plain, tasteless water. Then He instructed them to ladle some out and give to the master of the feast. One taste of this fabulous elixir and the master exclaimed that he'd never tasted anything so delicious, even commending the bridegroom for leaving the best for last. Did everyone there know what had happened? Probably not. But the disciples did, and they believed it was a miracle created by God.

Jesus chose a wedding, the uniting of two hearts in love, two families in harmony, to demonstrate His glory, and in doing so, turned the simple into the spectacular. Why? So people would believe in Him and what He can do, trust His goodness and unfailing love, and look to Him for help in all situations – the small and the great, the ordinary and the arduous.

What miracle are you looking for today? If you're wondering or waiting if you'll ever get your miracle, think of Job. Even Job, who experienced such devastating heartache, believed that God could perform miracles. Despite his catastrophic tragedies, while sitting in the dust and scraping his wounds with a piece of broken pottery, he bravely stated: *"He does great things too marvelous to understand. He performs countless miracles"* [Job 9:10].

That is what God does – every day. Don't give up. Keep praying. Keep believing. Keep looking to the generous hand of God. Your miracle is like a butterfly. First it is hidden in a chrysalis – dull and dusty – but then it's ready to burst forth into something beautiful, vibrant, perfect. It's coming. Wait for it. And wonder in it. Then share its abundance.

What no eye has seen

Miracles happen when God steps into a routine situation and makes it extraordinary. Have you wondered about miracles lately? Have you wondered if God is still in the miracle business? Have you been waiting for yours - and waiting and waiting? Have you heard what He's done in other's lives and wondered if God truly intervened or if it just happened by chance?

Sometimes our miracle meter is flat, isn't it? It doesn't seem to even flicker when we see things that are amazing. Well, today, we're going to relook at some of the miracles recorded in God's Word and see what He's doing in others around us – ordinary people like you and me for whom God stepped in and performed the impossible. Miracles are moments of the phenomenal waiting to happen. Paul explains to the Corinthians: *"No eye has seen, no ear has heard, and no human mind has imagined what God has prepared for those who love him"* [1 Corinthians 2:9].

This chapter looks at two of the physical miracles that Jesus accomplished. In this instance, Jesus had just come down from the mountain when a man riddled with leprosy stepped up to Him and fell to his knees before Him, begging to be healed [Matthew 8]. Unrepulsed by the horrid sores covering the man's body, Jesus reached out and touched the desperate man. This might have been the first human touch the man had received in years. In ancient times when someone contracted leprosy, they were forced to leave their family, friends, and community, often living in caves with others who'd also contracted the disease. To further their feelings of abandonment and isolation, whenever they went in public, they had to shout "Unclean! Unclean!" to warn anyone away from them and their hideous infection. It was a lonely, pain-filled life.

Thus, when Jesus reached out to the leper, He was showing him that he mattered. He was providing him His healing touch. Medical studies have shown significant relief from pain and anxiety, even healing of wounds through the miracle of touch. Other studies illustrate the potential benefit for those suffering from fractures and arthritis, while still others even suggest its healing influence in some cases of cancer. Certainly, Jesus, our Great Physician, knows the power of touch and so He reached out and touched this man who'd been ravaged emotionally and physically by his incurable disease.

But that wasn't all. The man asked if Jesus was willing to heal him. Did Jesus want to make him well? Did Jesus care enough for him to turn his life around? Yes, He did. With the utterance of one phrase from Jesus, the man's illness left him. His tumors and lesions disappeared. Even body parts that had been eaten away by the disease were restored.

Did the man question if this was a miracle? He didn't have to look at the miracle to confirm it. He could feel the abrupt change that came over his entire system. Surprisingly, after such a remarkable event, Jesus requested his silence. Why didn't He want the man to shout it out? To tell everyone about the miracle. Because Jesus knew what would happen. People would flock to Him for healing of their bodies but not their souls [Mark 1:45] and when the man did speak out that was exactly what occurred.

Jesus found He couldn't go anywhere without crowds of people following him. On this occasion recorded in Mark 2, He had returned to Capernaum and was preaching the Word. There were so many people who came to hear Him that there was no room left in the house. Even the doorway was blocked. But that didn't stop four faithful friends. Their companion was sick – even to the point of death. The disease had wasted him to the point that he couldn't even walk anymore. The four faithful friends knew they had to do something right away or their friend wouldn't survive. They could see death in his face. When they heard Jesus, the healer was back in town, they bundled up their friend and carried him to the place, but when they reached the house, they discovered such a crush of people that they couldn't get close to Jesus. What to do? They looked up and spied the roof. Hastily, they climbed the outside stairs to the flat thatched roof and began to dismantle it until they could lower their friend down before Jesus.

Can you imagine the people inside the house as thatch began to tumble down onto their heads? Can you imagine their irritation as they brushed off dried bits of grass and even the occasional spider? They probably even shouted up to the men to stop tearing apart the house, but that didn't deter the four friends. They weren't satisfied until they'd set their sick friend down in front of Jesus.

Was Jesus disturbed by this interruption? Not at all. Mark tells us that "*Seeing their faith, Jesus said to the paralyzed man, "My child, your sins are forgiven.*" [Mark 2:5] What an interesting statement. He saw their faith and forgave their friend. Even though the man was paralyzed, Jesus first concern was for his soul. Jesus knew healing the body would make little difference if the soul was still diseased, so He tackled that problem first. "*Your sins are forgiven.*"

The Bible often draws a connection between sickness and sin. I want to reassure you that this is not true in every case, lest people reading this may feel condemned because they are sick, but Hebrews 12:15 makes reference to the cost of bitterness and Jesus speaks to the man He heals on the Sabbath not to continue in sin [John 5]. Given that many doctors ask their patients if they are carrying any anxiety or anger that may contribute to ill health, there is certainly a correlation between our mental and emotional state and our physical health.

It was this concern that Jesus had for the man whose friends lowered him through the roof. But He was also concerned for the people around him. He knew that Pharisees were there who just came to challenge Him. The religious men, trained in the Tanakh and pious in their rituals of faith, wanted to find fault in Him for something. Jesus knew their thoughts and addressed their hostility and disbelief, but He also reassured the crowd that He had the authority to heal all manner of diseases and forgive all manner of sins. Then He spoke life to the paralyzed man, instructing him to stand and take his mat and return home to his family [Mark 2:11]. Immediately the man felt strength returning to his limbs; he found his legs could hold him upright and his hands could carry his mat. Thus, surrounded by his exuberant friends and astonished observers, he rose from his sick bed and elatedly walked home.

Did his heart change that day? Let's hope so. His friends believed in him enough to break apart a house and lower him down to Jesus. Jesus loved him enough to forgive his sins and heal him.

Both stories show us that Jesus is willing to heal our diseases as well as our hearts. We're never too untouchable that He won't reach out and lay His hands on us. We're never too sick that someone can't bring us to His throne of grace to receive His restoration.

Never tire of asking, never tire of seeking, never tire of reaching out to our Savior. His healing power still exists today. Just ask Art Sanborn. He'd been body surfing in Hawaii when a freak wave crashed him into the sand, crushing his vertebrae. Before he could think, the numbness started to take over and all feeling began to ebb from his legs. In the hospital, he was told the bad news that, with his kind of injury, it was unlikely he would ever walk again. But he believed in the power of prayer; believed in God's willingness to heal. And so, surrounded by the prayer of friends from around the world, he stepped off his bed. He couldn't feel his feet touch the floor, but they held him up; he couldn't feel his feet take one step after another, but they did. He is a walking miracle. Literally. God did the amazing miracle of touching his limbs, vertebrae, even his brain to help him walk again.

Truly we are fearfully and wonderfully made and marvelous are the works of God [Psalm 139:14]. Let's rejoice in His wonderful works and pray for the miracles of healing for our loved ones - and for ourselves. Like Art Sanborn discovered, Jesus still heals and saves.

The Humble in Heart

One of the best loved stories of miracles is the story of the Centurion and his servant. Perhaps it was his dedication to his long-time assistant that grabs our attention for who of us wouldn't like our boss to extend that depth of compassion. Perhaps it's the expression of faith that is so awe-inspiring. Whatever the reason, it is one of the stories of Jesus' miracles that we remember from our Sunday School days. In case you missed that lesson, you can read the story in your Bibles from either Luke 7 or Matthew 8.

When Jesus was met by the Centurion, he'd just completed a series of messages starting with the Beatitudes: Blessed are the poor, the hungry, the sorrowful, promising them God's goodness toward them. He then rebuked the wealthy, the shallow, the arrogant, warning them of what was to come. He followed this by explaining that we need to love our enemies, even those who curse or beat us. These were amazing instructions and ones that we still struggle to follow. Jesus proceeded to explain we weren't to judge others, but to forgive and assist them. He ended His powerful sermon by stating we were to build our lives on a firm foundation, for a house built on sand would crumble [Luke 6:49.]

Clearly the Centurion had built his house upon a rock. He'd dug deep and forged a solid foundation, committing his faith to the building of a synagogue and helping the Jewish people. He was the kind of person that Jesus had just been preaching about. He'd loved his enemies, and for a Roman soldier forced to live and work on the far reaches of the Roman kingdom, he had every reason to despise the Jews. Most of his people did. But not him. He'd embraced the people and their faith.

His background is significant to understanding and appreciating the lessons embedded in this story. As a centurion, he was a hardened soldier who'd earned his position by hard work and not family money or power. His role was an important peace keeping position in a turbulent region. Most Jews considered centurions violent beasts who enjoyed inflicting undeserved pain upon them, but this Centurion obviously didn't have that kind of reputation. He was known for his compassion and generosity, so much so that when Jesus came to town, the Jewish leaders came to Him to ask for His help, explaining that the Centurion's servant was deathly ill.

Undisturbed by the fact that He was being asked to enter the home of a Gentile, Jesus willingly went with them, but before he even got to the house, the Centurion's friends told Him not to trouble Himself further. It wasn't because the servant had died. Oh no, the Centurion didn't feel worthy to have Jesus enter his home. A Roman soldier who didn't feel worthy in the presence of a simple Jewish rabbi. How could this be? The Centurion's position, power and wealth were certainly much greater than Jesus', a poor carpenter cum itinerant teacher. Perhaps the Centurion knew something that others hadn't yet realized. This wasn't an ordinary man, but truly was the Son of God. He certainly believed that Jesus had supernatural power for he said that Jesus just had to say the word and his servant would be healed. What incredible faith. 'I don't need to see, to believe. You don't need to touch to heal, Jesus. Just say the word.' Like God spoke at creation or Jesus said to the storm or to the Gadarene, the Centurion understood the power of authority. A word spoken must be obeyed. No question, no delays. The Centurion believed that Jesus had that kind of authority.

Do you remember what I said Jesus had just been teaching? He'd spoken to the wealthy not to be selfish, shallow and arrogant. Here was a wealthy man who was the complete antithesis of those qualities. He may have been wealthy, but he was selfless, sincere and humble. He hadn't flaunted his wealth and authority or used his power to abuse others. Rather he'd built a firm foundation for his soul as exhibited by his works of generosity in funding a synagogue and giving to the poor. Even his humble refusal to have Jesus enter his house illustrated an exemplary character. He wasn't a mindless warrior, but a thoughtful, caring man who was aware of the needs of the people around him and graciously responded to them.

Was Jesus impressed? He was stunned. In all his travels he'd never seen such faith. Here was a man not raised on the oracles of God, not part of the covenant people, not of the line of Abraham, Isaac and Jacob. But his faith was greater than anyone else that Jesus had seen. Even his disciples. Wow! That's incredible faith. What did Jesus do? He acted accordingly. He used His authority to speak a healing word, and the Centurion's servant was restored at that moment. At that moment! Jesus spoke and His words accomplished what they were sent out to do as we are assured in Isaiah 55:11: *"It is the same with my word. I send it out, and it always produces fruit. It will accomplish all I want it to, and it will prosper everywhere I send it."* Humility seems to also play a major factor in this miracle story, suggesting that a humble heart pleases God. The Psalmists wrote of it [Psalm 18:27; Psalm 149:4], and the apostle Paul emphasized the connection in his letter to the Colossians [3:12].

What are we to learn about miracles from this story of the Centurion and his servant? We cannot go to Jesus with lots of fanfare and arrogance and expect Him to respond to our requests. Jesus explained that truth in His parable of the prideful Pharisee and the modest Tax Collector recorded in Luke 18. The garrulous Pharisee seemed assured that his prayers would be heard because he held such an important religious position, but the Tax Collector knew his penitent place before God and came to Him in humility. It's a humble heart that is heard by God [James 4:10]. Thus, let's be like the Centurion, acting as James [3:13] advises: *"If you are wise and understand God's ways, prove it by living an honorable life, doing good works with the humility that comes from wisdom"*. The Centurion showed us the way and look at the miracle that happened.

Even Nature Obeys

Life often seems to be full of storms. Your mom gets sick; your employer lays you off; your marriage is crumbling. All these things swirl around you like leaves in the wind and you can't seem to get your feet on the ground. Jesus understands when we will face times like this and shows us what He can do about it.

His answer is found in three gospels: Matthew, Mark and Luke. The Story in Mark [chapter 4] opens with Jesus teaching by the Lake. The crowd that gathered around him was hungry for answers and desperate for help; it was so large that He had to step into a boat to secure a lakeside podium. Still the crowds pressed against the water's edge to ensure they caught every word. From the swaying fishing boat, Jesus began to teach His life lessons: Parable of the Sower, Lamp on a Stand; the Growing Seed and the Mustard Seed, all parables relating to the Kingdom of God. Finally, evening came and the listeners, weary from the warmth of the sun and the stirring messages, began their long trek home.

Jesus, in turn, knew he had an appointment with a demon possessed man in Gedarene, and asked his fishermen friends to sail to the other side of the lake. Then he promptly lay down and fell asleep. But his friends weren't so fortunate. The wind picked up and the waves crashed over the boat. Although seasoned sailors, the disciples were unprepared for the suddenness and the ferocity of this storm and try as they might couldn't maneuver their small craft. Waves slashed against the boat and the disciples couldn't bucket out the water fast enough. They felt certain their fishing vessel was going to sink. Yet, despite the chaos, the pounding waves, shrieking winds and bellowing disciples, Jesus slept on seemingly undisturbed.

They clambered over to Him and roughly shook Him awake, shouting at Him for help. Slowly He uncurled Himself from His cramped position on the ledge of the boat, wiped the sleep from His eyes, and stood. Bracing His feet to steady Himself against the furious rocking of the boat, Jesus fearlessly faced the buffeting winds and mountainous waves. Paintings show Him raising His hands as if forcing back the wind and waves, but Scripture doesn't say that. Calmly He scolded the wind and waves, ordering them to settle down. The waves had obviously overstepped their mark. Perhaps Satan was trying once again to destroy Jesus and stirred the forces of nature which, truth be told, only had one Master [Psalm 148:7-10]. Whatever the situation, Jesus chastised the wind and waves severely for exceeding their set boundaries.

Did the wind and the waves listen to their Master? Immediately! To the disciples' complete amazement, the wind calmed to a gentle breeze and the waves glassed over. The rocking in the boat ceased. These men had seen Jesus heal the sick, lame and blind, saw Him feed thousands with a scrap of food, witnessed demons flee from His presence. But there was something about this miracle. Something amazing to watch nature in all its fury humble itself before a greater force - the living God.

Then Jesus turned to the disciples and asked: *"Why are you so afraid? Do you still have no faith?"* 'With all you have seen me do, with all that I have taught you, do you still not believe? Do you still not know who I am or what I am capable of?' Scripture tells us: *"They were terrified and asked each other, "Who is this? Even the wind and the waves obey him!"* [Mark 4:40]. They were overwhelmed with the evidence, amazed that wind and waves bow before Him. They thought they knew Him and what He could do, but they hadn't seen the half of it.

Is that the way it is with us? Life is swirling around us and the winds are blowing hard, threatening to sink our precarious little life boat. No matter how hard we try to bucket to stay afloat, we're sure we're going to drown. 'Jesus,' we cry, 'wake up. See my problems. They're too difficult for me and I can't keep up. I'm sinking.'

Peter tells us his story about such an experience in Matthew 14. Jesus had been teaching the crowd on the mountainside and in His compassion for His lost sheep had just performed the miracle of feeding the five thousand. At day's end, Jesus told the disciples to get into the boat and go the other side while He sent the people home. Tired but fulfilled He went up to pray and learned that His disciples were facing a treacherous storm. Jesus knew what He had to do.

He came to them, walking on the water. The disciples couldn't believe their eyes. Here was Jesus walking toward them. They were far from land, had faced a ferocious storm all night and now Jesus was striding across the waves as if He was on dry land. The waves didn't bother Him, the winds didn't disturb Him. He was coming to His children because they needed Him.

"It's a ghost," they said. They turned a miracle into superstition. The reality into myth. Jesus spoke to them: *"Take courage! It is I. Don't be afraid."* Peter, ever the dauntless one, the one speaking before thinking, replied: *"Lord, if it's you, tell me to come to you on the water."* {Matthew 14:26-28] Perhaps he needed to hear Jesus' voice. Maybe he needed some specific instruction so he would know what to do. Was he a man of faith? Not quite yet.

Jesus beckoned him forward. At the gesture, Peter stepped out of the boat and placed his feet firmly on the water. When his eyes were on Jesus, Peter stood on top of the water. But then he looked around, saw the lapping waves wash over his feet, felt the wind tearing at his hair and clothes and realized what he was doing was impossible. It wasn't natural for a man to walk on water. As these doubts gripped him, Peter began to slowly sink beneath the waves. First the water covered his ankles, then his knees, then up to his waist. In desperation he cried out for help. Jesus only had to stretch out His hand to pull Peter up beside Him, and the frightened fishermen clung to him like a limpet.

'Where is your faith, Peter? Why didn't you believe that if I called you, I would see you safely through', Jesus asked the trembling Peter.

Clutching to the strong arm of His Savior, Peter walked steadily with Him back to the boat and stepped in. Only then did the wind cease. No doubt Peter's legs were shaking as he collapsed onto the inside ledge of the boat. The rest of the disciples were equally stunned and dropped to their knees in worship, saying hoarsely: *"You really are the Son of God!"* [Matthew 14:33]

In these two miraculous accounts, Jesus proves that nature is no match for His power. He commands and nature obeys.

What seems too great for you today? What whirlwind has you in its grip? Recall these stories of what Jesus can do in the midst of our storms. Nothing need overwhelm us. Nothing need swamp our little boat. Even when we step out from its protection into dangerous waters, the winds and waves can't pull us under. Jesus is both our life boat and our life preserver. He will carry us through every storm, lift us above every wave, calm every tumult. Truly He is the Son of God!

Maybe Peter was thinking of his time with Jesus walking on the waves when he wrote: *"These trials will show that your faith is genuine. It is being tested as fire tests and purifies gold – though your faith is far more precious than mere gold. So when your faith remains strong through many trials it will bring you much praise, glory and honor on the day when Jesus Christ is revealed to the whole world."* [1 Peter 1:7]

May our faith, too, remain strong through every storm we face as we anticipate the miracle that will see us through. Then Jesus will be glorified in our victory.

Sharing Our Lunch

Have you ever been hungry? I'm not talking about a craving for something – Like 'I'm hungry for chocolate' or the tiny little cramp in our stomach that tells us that we've missed lunch. I'm talking about the 'I need to eat or I'm going to faint' kind of hunger. There were people on a hillside one very warm day who knew that feeling all too well. They'd heard the teaching, but more importantly they'd seen the healing. They wanted more. They needed more. The cramp of hunger wasn't just of the body, but of the soul. So they stayed right where they were.

The story of the feeding of the 5000 is recorded in all four gospels: Matthew 14:13-21; Mark 6:30-44; Luke 9:10-17; John 6:1-15 and you can read it in any one of them. Interestingly, in Matthew and Mark's record, the miracle occurs right after the beheading of John the Baptist. As sorrowful as Jesus was that His cousin was gone, as aware as He was that His messenger was dead, as sure as He was that the people would turn on Him one day very soon, Jesus still thought first of his listeners needs and not His own. He willingly accepted their discomfort and desperation and laid His own aside. Mark tells us that He saw this great crowd of people coming toward Him and He had compassion on them. Luke the physician explains that He welcomed them and spoke to them about the kingdom of God and healed the sick.

Always Jesus was giving, serving, loving. After a long day of this ministry, everyone was tired and hungry. The disciples noticed the weariness on every face, saw the gauntness etched into every cheek. Most were far away from home and needed to begin their journey now or they'd faint on the way. The disciples were also exhausted and longed for a quiet place to eat a much-deserved meal and thus, advised Jesus to send the crowd home. Basically, they were saying – 'Get rid of them Jesus – it's late and we all need to eat.' But Jesus had a better solution and instructed Philip to feed them.

You can almost see Philip's jaw drop. Feed – thousands. He wanted to serve the Master, but this was overwhelming. Before him stood a mob of hungry, tired people and he had nothing to give them, nor enough money to purchase even a crumb of food. Was Philip expecting a miracle -- apparently not – did he think that he was going to chew on a heavenly loaf of bread – not likely. None of the disciples exhibited any sign of possessing the mustard seed faith Jesus talked about in Matthew 17:20, but it didn't stop Him from doing the miraculous.

When Jesus asked the disciples to feed the multitudes, did they present Him with the dried loaf of bread they 'd brought with them? Not according to scriptural accounts. Perhaps the disciples had some bread stowed away in their back packs, but clearly the Bible tells us that if they did, they didn't offer it. Maybe they lacked the faith to think that their meagre offering could make a dent in feeding so many. They may have thought 'we've already sacrificed so much, we don't need to give anymore'. Whatever the case, it was a young boy who generously stepped forward and offered his meal of five small loaves and two tiny fishes. It certainly wasn't much, but like the widow's mite [Luke 21:1-4], it was all he had, and he offered what he could.

What happens next in this story is worth noting? Mark and Luke explain the careful organization Jesus provided the disciples, instructing them to seat the massive crowd on the grassy hillside, separating them into manageable groups of 50. It's likely He wanted the tired, hungry people to be at rest and not stampede when food was presented. It's also possible He wanted them to understand and appreciate that God was in their midst and answering the cry of their grumbling tummies.

Then Jesus prayed. But it wasn't to ask for a miracle. It was to thank His heavenly Father for it. He was already assured that it would take place. He was already anticipating the miraculous expansion of food that would fill every hungry soul. The food was successfully and peaceably distributed and all 5000 were contentedly full, so much so they couldn't eat another bite. Then Jesus directed his disciples to gather up the baskets of left overs so nothing would go to waste. We aren't told if they sent the left overs home with the needy or handed it out to the poor they met on the road, but certainly there was nothing left on the hillside. In an age of extravagance and waste this is a powerful message. Take what you have; share with others; then give even the leftovers away. Let nothing be squandered.

Were people aware of the miracle that they'd witnessed? You bet. They proclaimed Jesus a prophet and were ready to forcibly make Him their king. Anyone who could fill their physical hunger was just the person they wanted to rule over them, for they would never have to work a day in their lives again. They would always have enough to eat. But that wasn't the purpose of Jesus' miracle. He knew His kingdom was not of this earth and He had no desire to be an earthly king; thus, He drew away from the crowds to a quiet place to prevent this from happening.

As with every one of Jesus' miracles, there are so many lessons nestled in this story. Where shall we begin? The first is that Jesus saw their need. He knew they'd travelled far to find Him and that they could never make it back home without getting some food in their bellies. In the same way, Jesus is always keenly aware of what we need – both spiritually and physically – and responds precisely to that need.

Even though the disciples weren't expecting a miracle and were ready to tell the crowd to return home hungry, their lack of faith didn't prevent Jesus from providing the miracle that was needed. In the same way, our lack of faith doesn't prevent God from working – does this sound contrary to scripture – in some cases yes – but in this story, Jesus wasn't responding to their faith, but to the lack of it – to show them who He is and what He can do. Should we have faith? – absolutely – is God capable of working if we don't? – Yes! Paul writes:

"If we are unfaithful, he remains faithful, for he cannot deny who he is."
[2 Timothy 2:13]

Even though the disciples as adults had walked closely with Jesus and seen what He could do, it was a child that had the faith to believe and give. Faith always gives and a giving heart always has faith. Sometimes as adults we try to complicate things. 'I can't give because I won't have enough for myself', we rationalize. Or 'I can't give because it won't be enough anyway'. God didn't ask the little boy to do the math – 5 loaves – 5000 people. He just asked him to give and he did. Let us have faith like that. Let us demonstrate generosity with just that same willingness, and not discourage our little ones when they want to share. *"For the Kingdom of Heaven belongs to those who are like these children"* [Matthew 19:14].

Did you ever think that perhaps Jesus used this event to teach us how to organize food distribution programs? I really hadn't until I thought more of all the things He was trying to teach us in this event. He had the people sit down – so they wouldn't crowd around and, in their desperation, grab the food. He separated them into manageable groups to make the distribution easier. He showed us how to more easily and smoothly – without fuss or chaos – feed a large crowd of people. Having participated in food distribution programs myself that got out of hand, I can see the wisdom in Jesus' instructions.

Next – He gave thanks. He spoke to God believing that the miracle was already accomplished even before the first portion of bread or fish had been handed out. Can we imitate that response to God when we face a crisis – giving thanks for answered prayer no matter how impossible or seemingly unlikely – even before it happens, trusting that it will?

Then there is the abundance of provision. Nothing God ever does is miserly. He's always abundantly generous as witnessed in this story in which everyone ate until they were satisfied. It's similar to the story of manna where God provided daily food for the children of Israel [Exodus 16:17-19]. Then, too, everyone had enough and no one had too much. That's how God provides for us – satisfying our needs and ensuring we have just what we require.

Finally, with what He's given us, we should never be wasteful. On the hillside, the disciples collected twelve full baskets of leftover bread. Did they let it go to waste? – not likely because that's exactly what Jesus wanted to prevent. Undoubtedly Jesus fed the needy in the crowd or in the villages they passed. How then, should we act with the abundance that He's given us? We need to follow the example of this lesson as we are told in Ephesians 5:1: *"Imitate God, therefore, in everything you do, because you are His dear children. Live a life filled with love, following the example of Christ."* Therefore, be generous. Let nothing go to waste. Go through your closet and get rid of those extra clothes you never wear – the dishes, blankets or boots you never use. Give as you have received – generously, thoughtfully, sincerely.

There is also a caution in this story. The people, witnessing the provision of food to meet their physical needs wanted to forcefully make him their king. They wanted this miracle worker to take care of their needs every day, so they wouldn't have to any more. They didn't want to suffer the tyranny and poverty forced upon them by the Roman rulers. They wanted their lives to be easier. From this we must ask the question: Do we run after Jesus just because He is generous. Do we give so we can get back? I hope not, for later in John 6 – the same chapter that we started with, Jesus rebukes the people who are still trailing after Him. He knows they just want their physical needs met, but he wants to give them eternity. He explains: *"I am the bread of life. Whoever comes to me will never be hungry again. Whoever believes in me will never be thirsty."* [John 6:35]. Jesus used the miracle of the feast he prepared for the 5000 to teach this great eternal lesson. Believe in the One who is the true manna from heaven [John 6:58]; believe in the One who fills every hunger, every need. Believe in Him and we will hunger no more [Matthew 5:6].

Going Fishing

We seem to always be facing tax season, don't we? Either we're getting ready to pay it or have just covered the amount or look at our paycheck amazed at how much comes out each month. Some have even tried to devise ways not to pay it even though it's the law to do so, and those efforts never end well. Yet how many of us pray for God to help us with this necessary process of salaried life? It doesn't often cross our minds, does it? But one day, it did Peter's. As was so often the case, the religious leaders were trying to entrap Jesus. Surely, they thought, no one was as good as He was, especially when He made such outlandish claims as being the Son of God, Bread of Life, Good Shepherd.

Well in Judea it was once again tax season, and the required temple tax, the amount required by religious law, had to be paid. The temple tax, described in Exodus 30, is so named as it was to be used to care for the Tabernacle, was to be equally paid by everyone, rich and poor, and required as an atonement offering to the Lord. Because it was a mandatory payment and the religious leaders wanted to catch Jesus in the act of not following the prescribed laws, they accosted Peter on this point. Remember that Jesus often challenged the way that the laws of Moses were fulfilled, asking the Pharisees why they tithed herbs like mint and cumin yet didn't show justice and mercy [Matthew 23:23]. Jesus knew their hearts and understood that their interest was in their appearance of piety whereas they secretly wanted to protect their wealth from needy family members. Jesus addressed their lack of family commitment and generosity when He reminded them of their aging parents [Mark 7:9-13].

His chastisement bit into them. Like His writing in the sand [John 8:6] the Pharisees felt the weight of their selfish decisions. Moreover, they were tired of looking like fools before this itinerant carpenter cum teacher and wanted to seek their revenge against Him. If Jesus truly flaunted the law as He did with healing on the Sabbath or declaring Himself able to forgive sin, then it was likely He would refuse to pay the temple tax the Pharisees reasoned, so they questioned Peter [Matthew 17:24-27].

There are a host of lessons nestled into this small, seemingly insignificant miracle. It doesn't say 5000 were fed, or blind eyes could see, or lame legs could walk. Yet this miracle teaches us once again how to live godly in the world. First Jesus knows what Peter has been asked before they even have the conversation. This helps us to remember that before we speak, Jesus knows what's happened and what we're thinking. Even though Peter assures them that Jesus faithfully pays His taxes, he doesn't really know for sure. He certainly knows that they don't have the necessary funds to pay the tax. After all he hasn't been fishing lately because of all the travelling he's been doing with Jesus, a commitment which has left him a little short of cash.

Even so, Jesus knows what Peter has been doing. He knows the commitment and sacrifice Peter has made and wants him to understand that God, His Father, will take care of him. He asks him if the king's family pays tax. 'Of course not', Peter replies. 'That's right Peter. And you are in God's family, and the Father will take care of your costs as well,' Jesus answers him. Jesus also knows it's not yet time to be thrown into prison, judged or executed. He has more to do before He goes to the cross. In order to adhere to religious custom, Jesus advises Peter to "go down to the lake and throw in a line. Open the mouth of the first fish you catch, and you will find a large silver coin. Take it and pay the tax for both of us". [Matthew 17:27]

Peter was a fisherman and how else would he find the funds necessary to pay his taxes, but from the task he was trained to do. Yet it wasn't in the normal manner. He wasn't to bring in a boatload of fish. Just one. The fish that Jesus would send his way. The fish that had swallowed the coin necessary to pay the temple tax. How does Jesus expect us to pay our taxes? Is it not through the profession that He gives us? Through the job that He blesses us with. He may place an extra amount in our paycheck just when we need it or find some other miraculous manner to help us pay our taxes. We need only be ready for the miracle that God sends our way.

What about the fish that was heaven sent? In the Sea of Galilee there is a fish known as tilapia. They are also known as *musht* and have now been given the name St. Peter's fish as a result of this story. The males of this species are known to carry their young in their mouths. They also have a tendency to pick up tiny stones and shiny objects and carry them in their mouths. Perhaps it was one of these fish that God instructed to pick up the shiny coin that had fallen into the sea, just for such a time as this. In the same way, each of us have a responsibility in fulfilling God's purpose. From the tiniest fish to the biggest whale, each of us are called by God to accomplish His plans. Likewise, it doesn't matter how small or seemingly insignificant we are or how large and powerful. Each of us has a plan and a purpose in the Kingdom of God.

Well, you may ask: 'What are we to be obedient in'? Isn't it in following the laws of the land as well as the laws of God? As such we need to pay both our taxes to the government and our tithes to the Lord. Sometimes we chafe at this. My husband's sister was aggravated about having to fill out her income tax form. Why should she pay her taxes when she had so many needs, she fumed. When she challenged John, he told her about this story.

Begrudgingly she submitted her income tax return. Imagine her absolute joy when she received a large check back from the government. It was an unexpected, but much appreciated bonus that she'd never have received if she'd refused to fill out her taxes. Both the word of God and the example of John's sister shows us that we need to be obedient and leave the rest to God. The same goes with our temple tax – our tithe – the amount we're to cheerfully give to provide for the needs of our church. Without question, without remorse. For God has promised His provision when we obey Him in this instruction [Malachi 3:10-12].

How does this miracle end? When Peter pulled the fish from the water and discovered the coin, it could have been enough simply to pay for his own taxes. Jesus could have created His own coin or multiplied the coin just as He did with the bread. But He didn't. In the fish's mouth was enough to cover both of their temple charges.

What can we learn from this? The lesson here is similar to the lesson learned with the twelve leftover baskets collected from the multiplied bread and fish. Share the goodness of God's miracles with others. Whatever He has generously provided for you, give to others. Help them as God has helped you. Jesus explains it in this way in Luke 6:38: *"Give, and you will receive. Your gift will return to you in full— pressed down, shaken together to make room for more, running over, and poured into your lap. The amount you give will determine the amount you get back."* That's how He wants us to be – aware, watchful and ready to share His abundance with others.

As God always does, He wraps so much up in such a small package. In these four verses from Matthew 17, God teaches us to give the required amounts to God and country and share with others what He has given to us. How can we refuse such a simple yet compelling instruction?

A Miraculous Moment

It was another day of miracles for Jesus; yet He always personalized each encounter. Today He was on His way to heal Jairus' young daughter. She'd taken ill and the synagogue ruler in desperation rushed to find Jesus, and kneeling before Him, begged for His help. Jairus knew his daughter was on the brink of death and despite his best efforts she simply wasn't going to recover without supernatural intervention. There was simply no other hope but Jesus. Jairus had heard the reports of amazing miracles – the healing of blind eyes, paralyzed limbs, leprous sores. Nothing was too great or too advanced for the Master, so Jairus came with his earnest faith-filled request: *"My little daughter is dying,"* he said. *"Please come and lay your hands on her; heal her so she can live"* [Mark 5:23]. It was a brave statement for a Jewish religious leader, but his love for his daughter overrode any backlash he'd receive from his synagogue friends. Their criticism meant little in the face of his little girl's recovery.

Once again, Jesus didn't hesitate. All three gospel accounts in Matthew 9, Mark 5 and Luke 8 indicate that Jesus immediately turned and followed the anxious father through the crowd. But before he even got to Jairus's house, another miracle blossomed. A woman, ill for over a decade, waiting nervously for her moment with the Master, secretively reached out and grasped Jesus' robe.

Most of us know of this woman and have pondered her story. The gospels do not give us her name, but the early church called her Veronica when the story was told. For twelve long, painful, humiliating years she'd suffered. Luke, himself a physician, tells us that she'd searched desperately for medical cures, spending all her money on ineffective potions and lotions. Now her pockets were empty.

Worse than the financial cost was the emotional price she'd paid. For years her disease made her an outcast, forcing her to shout "Unclean" whenever she attempted to walk in the marketplace, if she even dared. Added to the rejection and isolation was the disgrace, knowing that others saw her illness as God's judgement for a sinful life, diagnosed her bleeding as the consequence of a secret wicked lifestyle [Numbers 5:11-31]. What scars she must have carried.

The very fact that she would risk exposure, risk coming into such close proximity to others without shouting out her shame, proved her desperation. Yet she wasn't brave enough to call out to Jesus as blind Bartimaeus had done [Mark 10:46-52]. She had no friends to push apart the crowd or rip through a roof like the paralytic man [Mark 2:1-12]. She wasn't courageous enough to believe that Jesus would stop for her. After all she wasn't an important man like Jairus - just a woman with a cursed disease. Yet within, there was a flutter of hope, a butterfly wing of faith that whispered: 'Only a touch, a tip of his hem. That's all it'll take'.

She didn't even feel that she needed to get his attention. She didn't even feel that He needed to speak over her life. She certainly didn't believe that He needed to touch her. In fact, what man save the doctors would want to touch a woman like her, unclean as she was with the filth of her disease? But she did believe that if she just touched His garment, just His garment, she would be made whole again. Matthew and Luke tell us that she inched her way close enough through the pressing crowd and stretched out shaking, straining fingers to touch His hem.

Have you thought about this gesture – grasping the hem of His garment. She didn't reach out and tap His shoulder, clutch His arm and even grasp the back of His cloak. She bent down, practically on her knees and touched the very bottom of His robe. It was a position of submission and surrender. A gesture that said, 'I'm not worthy to bother you, but maybe God's power will find me'. And as the tips of her fingers brushed His hem, she immediately felt healing course through her. Her weakness and the cursed flow of blood stopped. Any of us who have been ill know that terrible dragging feeling, that aching weariness, and in the case of Veronica she'd felt this for years. But now suddenly it was gone. Strength and energy surged through her; she could feel the flush of health filling her again.

Just as she knew that the bleeding had stopped, Jesus did as well. Just as she had felt His healing power released into her body, Jesus had felt the healing power released from His. He turned to the crowd and asked, *"Who touched my robe?"* [Mark 5:30]. The disciples froze, amazed the Master would ask such a ridiculous question in such a cramped space. But Jesus calmly waited and looked about the crowd. Trembling with fright, the woman stepped forward and dropped to her knees at His feet. In a quivering voice she described the events that led her to that moment. Told the horrified crowd of her humiliating disease, her failure to follow religious protocols, her brash approach of a holy man. But raising her head, she looked into the compassionate face of Jesus, her healer and in a clear firm voice announced: 'But my bleeding has stopped and I am completely cured'.

Jesus understood the anguish and torment she'd endured, realized her courageous action in seeking Him in a public place, knew the moment she'd received her miracle. His response: *"Daughter, your faith has made you well. Go in peace"* [Mark 5:34]. He called her "daughter". How this loving term of endearment must have healed yet another part of her. Not only was her body restored, but her soul as well. By His acceptance, He removed the stain of rejection and abandonment that she'd felt from the stigma of her disease. By His acknowledgement, He ensured her welcome restoration into the community. Through His admiration of her faith, He honored her spiritual fortitude. *"Go in peace. Your suffering is over."* [Mark 5:34]. With these words, not only was the ravagement of the disease erased, but the years of emotional trauma as well.

Did Jesus know He would meet this woman that day? I believe He did because He Himself has said that He knows all things [John

13:3]. He didn't want her hiding in the shadows any more. He wanted everyone around her to realize her human significance. Others may have rejected her and cast her out, but He did not. He wanted them to see that the power of God could enter her life, a poor, diseased woman, just as completely as it could enter theirs. He wanted them to know that He unconditionally loved her and that everyone – male, female, young and old, Samaritan, Roman and Jew –could reach out to Him for healing of any disease and sickness.

"Your suffering is over." How many of us today long to hear those words from the Savior? Whether it's ill health, financial struggles, or family sorrows, to hear that our time of pain is over is like discovering the passing from the chill of winter into the warmth of spring [Song of Solomon 2:11-13].

What part of this message is for you today? Have you, like Veronica, heard that Jesus can do miracles? Do you need to push aside all doubt and fear and, in submission and surrender, touch just the edge of His garment and say, 'I believe that You can bring healing and recovery to my life'? Do you need to step out of the shadows and testify of His miracles in your life? Does Jesus need to restore your body and soul through His generous display of love and mercy?

Whatever you need today, I pray that you, too, reach out and touch the One who loves you best and most and let Him heal you.

Seeking Mercy

Does Jesus love everyone? Have you ever asked that question? Perhaps He loves children and the elderly more than teenagers or adults. Or maybe you think He loves those from a particular country more than He loves those from another. Maybe you've even thought that He prefers people of a particular ethnicity more than another.

Our hearts are always wounded when we think, even for a minute, that God loves someone because of their age or innocence, their nationality or race more than us. That's why when we read the story in Matthew 15 or retold in Mark 7 that we begin to wonder if indeed God does have favorites and we just aren't one of them. Here was a desperate mother crying out to Jesus for help. Her child was ill. Who cared if she was a Gentile from an area with a long history of hatred toward Jews? But Jesus ignored her. Like Jairus, the Jewish leader with a sick daughter, she came to Jesus for help. Yet unlike Jairus' request, Jesus didn't immediately rush to aid the woman and her daughter. No, horror of horrors, He did nothing. Didn't acknowledge her, give her a tender look or compassionate touch. He simply pretended she wasn't there.

Many of us may have accused Jesus of just such a response. We have come to Him crying out for help and felt like He's ignored us. His silence to our pleas has been deafening. We may have even given up and turned away ourselves. But the Syro-Phoenician woman didn't do that. She couldn't give up. Her daughter was too sick and she knew

He was the only one who could help. In desperation she pleaded for His merciful intervention [Matthew 15:22]. Her mother's heart hoped the needs of a sick child would soften His heart.

When reading the Scriptures, we often find the disciples disappoint us, don't they? Like when the mothers asked Jesus to bless their children in Mark 10. The disciples wanted to send that noisy rabble of babbling mothers and chattering children away because Jesus was too busy for such unimportant people. They wanted to do the same with the Gentile woman telling Jesus: *"Tell her to go away." "She is bothering us with all her begging."* [Matthew 15: 23] Yet it was their words of dismissal that prompted Jesus to turn to her.

How many reading this message have received mistreatment from a church leader, be it a pastor or someone else in church leadership? Maybe the words that they've spoken have wounded you to the point that you've turned away from the church and God. You considered their attitude as representative of how God thinks of you, an attitude that made you feel small and worthless, and you said 'No more! If that's how God feels about me then I don't need Him either'. But wait! I'm telling you that there is more to her story - and yours. Let's see what it is.

Jesus stopped then and spoke to her at last, but it still isn't the words that you'd expect. He says: *"I was sent only to help God's lost sheep—the people of Israel."* [Matthew 15:24]. Was He telling her that she wasn't worthy of His love or care or time? Was He saying that He wouldn't stoop to heal someone from her region, or of her nationality? That the Father wasn't concerned for someone from her area? We may recall what He instructed the disciples when He sent them to minister [Matthew 10: 5-8]. Perhaps the disciples were remembering this instruction and forgetting the time that Jesus healed the Centurion's servant [Matthew 8] or healed the demon-filled man in the Gentile region of Gerasene [Mark 5] or ministered to the Samaritan woman at the well [John 4]. Clearly Jesus had no intention of cutting anyone off from the offer of salvation no matter what their nationality. In His nighttime visit with Nicodemus, Jesus clearly explained that people from across the globe were loved by the Heavenly Father [John 3:16]. Last time I looked the world included everyone – from every tribe, nation, creed and tongue.

So why did He challenge this woman so relentlessly at such a sensitive time. For one thing, there'd been a long history of animosity between the Gentiles and the Jews, and although they were descendants of Noah's grandson [Genesis 10:32], they didn't worship God. Over the many centuries, their godless ways had been a bane to the Israelites and there were constant wars and divisions over faith and land between these two people groups. Anyone that listens to the news is aware that these grievances are still not forgotten, let alone forgiven and like the spiritual testing of the Samaritan woman at the well, Jesus was testing the Syro-Phoenician woman to see the nature of her heart. Thus, when He challenged her that He was sent only to the lost sheep of Israel, she didn't hesitate, but kneeled before Him and pleaded again: *"Lord, help me!"*

Jesus' response would make any one of us wilt in shame: *"It isn't right to take food from the children and throw it to the dogs."* But this earnest mother still didn't give up. Nor did she become belligerent and throw back in His face words of rage and hatred. No, she answered in heart-felt humility and gentleness. She didn't resist His definition of "dogs" but admitted that according to Jewish standards that is what they called her. *"That's true, Lord,"* but the rest of her answer illustrates her humble heart: *"but even dogs are allowed to eat the scraps that fall beneath their masters' table."* [Matthew 15:27]

What incredible meekness? She laid down everything. She didn't hold onto her nationality as if it were a badge of greatness. She didn't hold onto the years of prejudice and intolerance. She came to Him, knowing that He had the power to make her daughter well. The issue of nations, kings, and historical prejudice didn't matter in the face of Jesus. Her humble answer removes all sense of pride [Proverbs 16:18]. It's as if she is saying: 'You're right Jesus. I am nothing. I don't deserve your touch, but it doesn't matter who I am – it only matters who You are. You are the Master and I have come to Your table'. He has heard all He needs to hear; seen all He needs to see. Once again Jesus sees in a Gentile such great faith that He is overwhelmed: *"Dear woman,"* Jesus said to her, *"your faith is great. Your request is granted."* And her daughter was instantly healed." [Matthew 15:28]

How many times have we blustered: 'God, why don't you do this for me? Look at me. Look at all I've done for you. Look at my faithfulness. Look at my giving, my church attendance, my kindness, my goodness, or even my spiritual pedigree – parents who always went to church, husband a pastor, church or ministry leader. Why won't you answer my prayer?' Jesus doesn't need us to give an account of our worthiness to receive His help. He only wants to see our humility [Proverbs 22:4]. Just like He witnessed in the Syro-Phoenician woman.

Certainly, He wants us to realize that we're all equal in His sight. Perhaps in preparation of this incidence, He told the disciples in John 10:16 that His flock comprised sheep from other folds, not just theirs. Like the Syro-Phoenician woman, all His children, regardless of their ancestry or origins, will hear Him and, together, with Him as their Shepherd, they will be one.

We are those other sheep. He's calling us and listening for our cry. We mustn't give up because it seems as if He's not listening. He may be wanting to see our persistence as shown by the righteous widow in Luke 18. He may want to see us pressing through the crowd like the woman with the issue of blood described in Mark 5. He may want to see that our heart is fixed on Him and no one else [Hebrews 12]. The important thing is: Don't give up. Keep calling on Jesus for He answers every cry for help [Matthew 7:7,8].

Touched by Jesus

Jesus often healed on the Sabbath. He wasn't daunted by the rage of the Pharisees. He simply saw a need, knew what He was to do and did it. The story from Luke 13:10-13 is just such an event. An elderly woman, still faithful in her prayers, was seated in the women's section of the synagogue. Jesus noticed the earnest bend of her head but could also see the bowing of her spine that prevented her from looking up into His face. He knew that over the last twenty years her countenance had sunk lower and lower, forcing her to face the ground. It had been so very long since she'd felt the warmth of the sun on her cheeks or looked into the eyes of her grandchildren. His compassion stirred. He wasn't daunted by the longevity of her ailment or the holy place in which they stood. Rather it urged Him onward. He called her forward, speaking softly to her words of comfort and affirmation and then gently reached out and laid a warm hand on the curvature.

Suddenly she straightened. No creaking of bones or straining of muscles just a huge smile cresting a weathered face. The room gasped in unison and then angry murmurs began as the leaders shouted Him down. Jesus was incensed at their unfeeling criticism and reminded them that they fed even their work animals on the Sabbath yet had the audacity to complain when He freed a child of God on this holy day. Now it was their turn to hang their heads in shame for their faithless hypocrisy.

Let's review the characters in this story. Imagine, for instance, if you were this woman. You have gone to seek God as you have done throughout these long eighteen years, despite the illness that has bent your body. For all those years, for 216 months, 936 weeks, and 6570 days you have not been able to look anything in the eye but an ant on the ground. You have not been able to lift a child, hold a decent conversation with someone, or find one pain-free moment for your aching back. What a long, dreary, painful existence. Still, this woman worshipped. Still, she chose to go to synagogue to hear the Word and sing the hymns. She didn't go that day because she'd heard a great teacher was in town. She didn't go because she thought a miracle was going to happen to her. She went because this was her habit. Despite her infirmity, she was a worshipper.

Jesus must have seen this because, once again, in the midst of a crowd of people, He called a single person forth and addressed her personally. Then He touched her, someone He knew hadn't received little physical tokens of affection for a very long time. Immediately her entire life changed. One moment she was bent double, and the next she felt her spine stiffen, her muscles contract, and she straightened to stand erect. As Paul directed the Corinthians, this woman was literally able to *"Stand firm in the faith"* [1 Corinthians 16:13]. It was her day for a miracle.

How did she respond? Exuberantly. She was a faithful worshipper in her infirmity, and she was a worshipper when her healing came. Her life testifies to the importance of exhibiting a grateful heart in all situations and at all times. Three hundred and seventy-seven times in the New Living Translation we are told of the power of praise and Psalm 34:1 tells us to praise Him continually. This was the nature and life of this woman. It's unlikely that she knew this was her day for a miracle, yet she chose to praise regardless of her position.

But others, witnessing this miracle, were unimpressed, even angry that it occurred in this place at this time. 'Surely', they thought, 'church isn't the place for a miracle; the Sabbath isn't the time for God to show up.' They tried to use Scripture to bring Jesus in line, recounting the creation story of Genesis in which God worked for six days and then rested. Even Moses taught this [Exodus 20:8]. But Jesus wasn't going to stand for His Word to be misapplied or misunderstood. Furthermore, He reminded them as He did when He wrote on the sand when they wanted to stone the woman caught in adultery that He knew their deeds [John 8:1-11]. He knew that everyone there in some form or another worked on the Sabbath day. Probably He could point to the man making the complaint and say 'didn't you just lead Old Betsy, your donkey, to water this very morning.'

He also wanted to make sure the woman didn't suffer any repercussions for being healed on the Sabbath. After all the religious zealots had ousted a man Jesus had healed on the Sabbath already [John 9]. He made His position clear: *"This dear woman, a daughter of Abraham, has been held in bondage by Satan for eighteen years. Isn't it right that she be released, even on the Sabbath?"* [Luke13:16]. He was reminding them that this woman belonged to the same spiritual and tribal family that they did. Her infirmity, as so many believed in those days – and even in ours – didn't make her repelled by God or cast out of the family of faith.

In fact, her infirmity brought glory to God as across generations people would read of her healing and rejoice in what Jesus did, no matter the disease, no matter its duration. Just as with Job against whom for a season Satan was able to work his strategies of pain and disease, in the same way this woman experienced almost two decades of illness. Why so long? Why so painful? Like the woman with the issue of blood, we don't know the why, but we do know the result. In both cases Jesus healed them completely and restored the infirm to a whole and healthy relationship with society, providing them a place of recognition and respect for their great faith. This steadfast woman shows us how to persevere even if we don't know when or if our healing will come; her faithfulness urges us to hope healing will become our reality but worshipping even if it doesn't [Hebrews 11:1,2].

In addition, He wanted them to know that, although Satan had been allowed to keep her in sickness for eighteen long years, that at last his dominion over her physical body was over. The Great Physician had set her free. And those He sets free are free indeed as Jesus informs us in John 8:36, and those who are bent will straighten [Psalm 146:8].

What do we learn from the critics in the crowd? Through them we see again the importance of having a clear understanding of the Word of God [2 Timothy 2:15]. They were obviously quoting scripture but applying it poorly to the situation [Romans 12:2]. Certainly, God wasn't saying do nothing on the Sabbath and above all never lift your finger to help someone on that day. Rather He vehemently pointed out that any day is right to pray for someone's well-being, to seek their health and help them achieve it.

What was the result of this event? Certainly, that this long-suffering woman was healed. But there was more. Those who wanted to discredit Jesus, who wanted to misguide the people in the ways and character of God, were put to shame. How did the rest of the people respond? Without question, they were ecstatic [Luke 13:17]. God was in their midst, exulting the humble, and humbling the prideful [Proverbs 3:34].

What does this miracle teach us? Firstly, that individually we need to praise Him even in our pain. Persevere even when our suffering is extended. Secondly, we need to understand God's Word and apply it correctly to our lives and not criticize God when He does the miraculous. Lastly, we are to join with others in enthusiastically praising God when we witness Him stepping into our reality and doing the impossible. This story tells us clearly that Jesus wins over the enemy in every situation. That's enough reason in itself to rejoice every single day.

Our God is Greater

One thing we see in Scripture and hopefully through this book is that the miracles of Jesus are comprehensive, covering every aspect of our lives from the financial, as seen in the story of the coin tucked inside the fish so that Peter and Jesus could pay their temple tax [Matthew 17:24-27], to the physical with the feeding of the five thousand and four thousand, illustrating that Jesus is our eternal Bread of Life who can meet our physical needs [John 6:1-14], or the calming of the storm [Mark 4:35-41] showing that whatever calamity we are facing, Jesus can bring peace to it. In all these cases, Jesus saw the people, understood their need and answered it.

That's the important part of reading the miracles of Jesus: to realize again all that He can do and that our concerns are His concerns. We are going to turn our attention to another aspect of the miracles of Jesus to see how He touches our lives in meaningful ways to transform and to heal. I have no doubt that there isn't one of us reading this that doesn't need God to do some form of healing in our lives or for someone we love.

Today's study has us look at the vast number of times Jesus heals people who are oppressed by the devil. Now I understand that this may be a frightening topic and it's certainly often misunderstood, but because Jesus concentrates on people needing His intervention in this area, it's definitely an aspect of His miracles that we want to look at. Matthew describes five incidents in his gospel.

In Matthew 9, we read that it had been a very busy day for Jesus. He'd been called to the house of Jairus to heal his daughter who had in fact died of her illness. Before Jesus could even reach Jairus' house, a woman who'd been bleeding for twelve years, reached out just to touch His garment and discovered that her bleeding immediately stopped. After acknowledging her importance as a person and speaking with her about her faith, Jesus then proceeded to Jairus' home where, despite the mockery of those who couldn't see the point of Jesus' coming, He nonetheless raised Jairus' daughter from the dead much to the great rejoicing of her parents and the awe of His disciples. After leaving the house, two blind men called out for His help, and in their persistence even followed Him into a house. Seeing their determination, Jesus asked them first about their spiritual condition: *"Do you believe"* [Matthew 9:28]. Without hesitation they affirmed their faith. Satisfied that they could spiritually see, Jesus then touched their eyes and instantly their physical sight was restored.

Can you imagine the buzz of excitement that stirred the area, one healing after another of amazing proportions? Perhaps, after hearing of these incredible healings, friends were motivated to bring a man to Jesus who could not speak. Matthew [9:32] describes the man as demon-possessed. Undeterred by this type of illness or its cause, Jesus simply drove out the demon, releasing the man's ability to speak. In this very busy day, Jesus moved smoothly from healing the woman of a long-standing illness, to raising the dead, to opening blind eyes and then freeing someone from a spirit of muteness.

Three chapters later in Matthew 12, we read of another similar situation. Jesus was again brought a man who is blind and mute, disabilities we are told were caused by a demon. As before, Jesus touched the man and immediately the man could see and talk. Sadly, just as in the previous healing, the Pharisees, instead of praising God for the miracle, accused Jesus of being demon-possessed Himself stating that: *"No wonder he can cast out demons. He gets his power from Satan, the prince of demons."* [Matthew 12:24]. Jesus did not allow such blasphemy and instructed them that if He could free people from the influence of a demon, God had come to them [Matthew 12:28]. Jesus stated emphatically that His power was greater than anything Satan attempted.

A few chapters later in Matthew 15 we meet up with the Syro-Phoenician woman whose daughter was also tormented by a demon and once again Jesus healed her. This is followed two chapters later in Matthew 17 by the appearance of another desperate parent whose son had seizures so severe that he fell into the fire and the water. He asked the disciples to help but found their efforts unsuccessful. Jesus was concerned by their lack of faith, but still turned to the boy and healed him by admonishing the evil spirit who left, leaving the boy fully restored.

These stories of healing pale in comparison to the first one Matthew tells in Matthew chapter 8. Jesus was once again performing miracles of incredible proportions. Leprosy was healed, as was the Centurion's servant and Peter's mother, and the rocky seas were calmed. In this telling of the visit to Gadarenes, it was two demon-possessed men that exited the tombs. Their violent behavior had prevented many from going near them, but immediately upon seeing Jesus, the demons within squirmed. *"Why are you interfering with us, Son of God? Have you come here to torture us before God's appointed time?"* [Matthew 8:29] They knew their season of power was over for the King of Kings had come and begged Jesus to send them into pigs. Jesus calmly commanded them to leave and the men were freed while a herd of two thousand pigs sped off a cliff.

Each of these situations relate to Jesus healing those defined as demon-possessed. Jewish culture didn't doubt the existence of demons or their effect on people's lives. They recognized the possible symptoms: blindness, muteness, seizures, violent anti-social behavior. I am not suggesting that in contemporary society that all these types of maladies are demon related. Rather, I am simply looking at what Scripture says and what Jesus does. Can Satan harm us body and soul? I think we all believe that he can for he is out to 'kill, steal and destroy', but Jesus promises *"My purpose is to give them a rich and satisfying life"* [John 10:10] and that's what's most important.

Scripture does not tell us how each person was ensnared by Satan. It appeared Judas was trapped by his greed [John 12:6]. Perhaps the Gentile woman's daughter was influenced by the idol worship of her mother as described in Psalm 106:36-39. Peter, it seems, was swayed by his personal desire that Jesus avoid the cross [Matthew 16:22]. Jesus was firm and abrupt in His response: *"Get away from me, Satan! You are a dangerous trap to me. You are seeing things merely from a human point of view, not from God's."* [Matthew 16:23] We are advised to remember this response should we ever receive counsel that appears completely contrary to the Word of God, or the direction of the Holy Spirit. It may well be the enemy trying to dissuade us from what God truly wants us to do.

The important thing to remember is that Satan can never attack, torment or influence someone without God's permission and the assault may well be because He loves and trusts us so much. Certainly, this was the case with Job who was mercilessly attacked by the enemy despite his purity of heart. Yet God only allowed the enemy to go so far in his onslaught against him [Job 2:6] before He intervened [Job 42:10-17].

Indeed, Paul tells believers how to prepare themselves for the enemy's attacks in Ephesians 6, explaining in detail the comprehensive battle armor we are to wear. Undoubtedly, we need to prepare ourselves, yet we don't have to dwell on the enemy or be overcome by his efforts against us. In fact, James 4:7 instructs us how to defeat the enemy; if we humble ourselves, we're putting God first and the devil has no place when God is on the throne of our hearts. Jesus has shown us that no one can stand against Him. God always prevails. Whatever you're facing today, know that He will be victorious in your life as well.

The Light of His Glory

One of the most wondrous miracles of Jesus is His transfiguration. The story is recounted in Matthew 17, Mark 9, and Luke 9. By showing them a glimpse of His heavenly glory, Jesus hoped it would prepare His disciples for the horrors of the cross. 'Who am I? He'd asked, wondering if they could articulate His true nature. Without hesitation, Peter answered: *"You are the Messiah, the Son of the Living God,"* [Matthew 16:16]. Jesus was thrilled. Someone knew Him for who He was. In response, Jesus pronounced a blessing on Peter, giving him a new name, a new purpose and a new anointing [Matthew 16:17-19]. Wow that's heady stuff – especially for someone like Peter, a simple fisherman who'd set aside his livelihood, even his entire life, to follow Jesus.

Yet when Jesus went on to explain His journey to the cross, Peter was unprepared for that future. He only heard about the suffering and couldn't comprehend the resurrection. It had no frame of reference for him, so he rebuked Jesus, forbidding that heaven and earth had this future for his Lord. He and his friends needed Jesus. There were too many things they didn't know or understand, too many things they still couldn't do. Jesus couldn't die and leave them alone. Not now. Surely.

But Jesus wanted to help them understand what this would mean – what His heavenly glory looked like. Thus, He took Peter, James and John up to a mountain and there revealed Himself to them. Peter, the one Jesus told would receive keys for the Kingdom of Heaven and the gates of Hades would not prevail against it, James, the brother of John, who would be one of the first martyrs [Acts 12] and John, the beloved who would record the true nature of Jesus [John 1:1-5].

Jesus took them with Him for a time of reflection and revelation. It was then His appearance transformed and His clothes became as bright as a flash of lightning [Matthew 17:2]. Transfiguration refers to the complete change of form or appearance into a more beautiful or spiritual state. For Jesus this was a reality – an eternal spiritual and physical state of being, but it foretells the potential for our own spiritual transfiguration through the power of the Holy Spirit when our own likeness and garments will be transformed.

Nor was Jesus alone in His mountaintop moment. Moses and Elijah joined Him, also appearing in glorious splendor. Had Moses not beheld a heavenly sight when the angel of the Lord appeared to him in flames of fire from within a bush [Exodus 3]? Had Elijah not been taken up in a whirlwind when a chariot and horses of fire appeared as his supernatural transport [2 Kings 2]? While they lived on earth, their role was to act as law-giver and prophet, delivering the word of God to His people.

What did they speak to Him about? Luke 9 explains they were discussing Jesus' death, which He was about to accomplish in Jerusalem. The focus of His mission was clear. He was the Lamb of God who would take away the sins of the world and nothing could deter Him from that goal.

Peter, as always, was the first to react, but, like many impulsive people he didn't really know what he was saying. *"Master, it's wonderful for us to be here! Let's make three shelters as memorials—one for you, one for Moses, and one for Elijah"* [Luke 9:33]. He's referencing the Feast of Booths, an appointed festival explained in Leviticus 23:34-42. This Feast was a joyous celebration commemorating what God had delivered them from and brought them in to. Perhaps Peter spoke prophetically of the joyous celebration every believer would experience when God delivered them from the kingdom of darkness and brought them into the kingdom of His glorious light [Ephesians 5:8,9].

Before anyone else could speak, God's voice from Heaven called out: *"This is my Son, my Chosen One. Listen to him!"* [Luke 9:35] By this declaration, the Father was not only declaring that Jesus was His Son, but that He was with them, and that Jesus' teaching overshadowed the Law and the Prophets. As such, we are to listen to Him for He has the words of Life [John 6:63].

We recall that the Father also spoke at Jesus' Jordan baptism where He also declared: *"This is My dearly loved Son, who brings Me great joy" [Matthew 3:17]*. We see here that when Jesus' anointed ministry began, His Father declared Jesus His Son whom He greatly loved. Now as Jesus' earthly mission drew to a close, the Father once again acknowledged His Son, but exhorted those present to listen to Him. By saying this, the Father was confirming what Jesus instructed the crowd in Mark 7:14. Peter also admonished his listeners at Pentecost to listen as he spoke about Jesus [Acts 2:22].

Later John would write of the transfiguration in John 1:14, and Peter would record the account in 2 Peter 1:16-18. In this miracle, we see a glimpse of the cross – the journey that Jesus was determined to complete on our behalf. Further we see the wonder of His eternal glory – His appearance and garments brilliant as the sun as described in Revelation 1:12-16. Yet we are promised that by overcoming the challenges of this earthly life that we, too, will be given heavenly garments [Revelations 7:9]. But, you may ask, how do we overcome? Paul promises that it is by acknowledging and recognizing the Beloved Son of God and listening to Him [Romans 10:9].

The wonder is that we can let the miracle of this transfiguration take place in our lives every single day. We can let the power of His light and His glory transform us as Paul explains in his letter to the Corinthians: *"For God, who said, "Let there be light in the darkness," has made this light shine in our hearts so we could know the glory of God that is seen in the face of Jesus Christ"* [2 Corinthians 4:6]. May His light shine in our hearts today.

I have seen the King

The prophet Isaiah foretold one of the most amazing miracles ever recorded: the crucifixion and resurrection of Jesus Christ. Isaiah was birthed within a royal family and his prophetic words guided four different rulers: Uzziah, Jotham, Ahaz and Hezekiah. Despite the growing idolatry around him, Isaiah remained faithful, listening and obediently sharing the words God spoke to his heart. His declaration of God as he witnessed Him in all His greatness and holiness not only humbled him but weighted him with his own sense of unworthiness and inadequacy [Isaiah 6:1-5].

But as God has always done, He did not leave Isaiah in that state of despair. He showed his eternal mercy and cleansing power [Isaiah 6:6,7]. Each of us who have allowed these verses to permeate our hearts have breathed a sigh of relief to know that all we've spoken, thought and done have been removed by a touch from the Lord's loving hands. And once cleansing and restoration has taken place, purpose is infused into our lives. As with Isaiah, God does it so subtly that we don't even realize we've answered the call. This is what happened to Isaiah: *"Then I heard the Lord asking, "Whom should I send as a messenger to this people? Who will go for us? I said, "Here I am. Send me."* [vs 8]. Here I am, send me! It's the natural response to God who cleanses, who comforts, who restores. 'If you need me Lord, I will go'. Then the instruction comes as seen in Isaiah 6:9: "Go!" But God warned him that the people he spoke to wouldn't listen or change. What a tough ministry. Isaiah was daunted and even more overwhelmed when God explained how long they'd reject his message and the tragic consequences of their rebellion described in Isaiah 6:11,12.

With such a bleak picture of the future, did Isaiah refuse the Lord's call? Did he say, 'Lord if you don't give me more than this, I won't do it. Remember I'm from the royal family; wealth, power, position, status are mine. I shouldn't have to take on such a thankless job.' No, he didn't. Humbly he accepted it, embraced it, pursued it and because he did we have words that throughout the centuries have comforted, encouraged, counselled and directed people searching for answers and hope, like these in Isaiah 40: 31 *"But those who trust in the LORD will find new strength. They will soar high on wings like eagles. They will run and not grow weary. They will walk and not faint."* Who of us cannot breathe these words and feel God's strength fill us once more?

God, our Father knew that would be so, just as He knew we would need prophetic words to assure us that throughout eternity He intended to send His Son to die for us and reconcile us to Himself. Thus, we have Isaiah and his obedience to thank for the prophetic words we are going to look at today. Words that speak directly of a Savior born centuries after they were spoken, but whose life, ministry and sacrifice are foretold and recorded by a man surrendering to the will of God. Let's look to see what he told us.

Isaiah 53 calls us to listen, learn, and live. Satan may come as an angel of light [2 Corinthians 11:14], with beauty and charisma, but Jesus comes as one of us, a humble servant, a simple carpenter, to draw us to God, not with His majestic countenance but with His compelling message of love and salvation, His healing touch of restoration and wholeness.

But for all of this, He would still face rejection as Isaiah tells us: *"He was despised and rejected— a man of sorrows, acquainted with deepest grief. We turned our backs on him and looked the other way. He was despised, and we did not care"* [Isaiah 53: 3]. We can hear in these verses the crack of the whip and the shouts of the enraged determined to see him die.

The King James version, with which we are likely more familiar, describes in detail what would happen to Jesus. *"Surely he hath borne our griefs, and carried our sorrows: yet we did esteem him stricken, smitten of God, and afflicted. But he was wounded for our transgressions, he was bruised for our iniquities: the chastisement of our peace was upon him; and with his stripes we are healed."* [Isaiah 53:4,5]

Luke writes the fulfillment of these words in chapter 23 and Mark describes his flogging in chapter 15, but these brief verses don't capture the horror of the event. Thirty-nine times the wicked pottery shard tipped cat-o-nine-tails slashed across his bare back, and His innocent blood seeped into the ground. Despite the brutality of his executioners, Jesus spoke not a word in his defense just as Isaiah foretold: *"He was oppressed and he was afflicted, yet he opened not his mouth: he is brought as a lamb to the slaughter and as a sheep before her shearers is dumb, so he openeth not his mouth"* [Isaiah 53:7 KJV]. Mark fills in the details, recording the actual event in Mark 14.

Isaiah continues to foretell Jesus' execution in painful detail: *"Unjustly condemned, he was led away. No one cared that he died without descendants, that his life was cut short in midstream. But he was struck down for the rebellion of my people"* [Isaiah 53:8]. Paul explains the purpose of His sacrifice in Colossians 1:22 *"Yet now he has reconciled you to himself through the death of Christ in his physical body. As a result, he has brought you into his own presence, and you are holy and blameless as you stand before him without a single fault."*

Isaiah, seeing the unseen, writes of Jesus' innocence and death in 53:9, while Luke provides the event as witnessed by those present, describing the criminals crucified beside Him and the grave provided by wealthy Joseph of Arimathea [Luke 23:32,52-53]. Isaiah's concluding verses are fulfilled in several New Testament passages such as Romans 4:25 and 8:34.

Nor is Isaiah the only one who foretells the suffering of Jesus. The psalmist also anticipated Jesus suffering in Psalm 22. This psalm was written 1000 years before Jesus went to the cross, but its words ring with amazing accuracy to events that could only have been orchestrated by the hand of God. We read of His anguish as He cries with struggling breath: *"My God, my God, why have you abandoned me? Why are you so far away when I groan for help"* [vs.1] which were the exact words Jesus spoke as He hung on the cross. *"Eli, Eli lema sabachthani? My God, My God why have you abandoned me?"* [Matthew 27:46]. Those around Him did not understand the prophetic meaning of these words or His miraculous fulfillment of them in the midst of His suffering, but as we read them today we see the connection between Old Testament prophecy and New Testament fulfillment.

The Psalmist saw as it were His strength waning and thirst clawing at His throat and wrote for Him who did not yet speak: *"My strength has dried up like sunbaked clay. My tongue sticks to the roof of my mouth. You have laid me in the dust and left me for dead."* [Psalm 22:15]. John then recorded Jesus' hoarse whisper [19:28], which prompted the soldiers to bring Him tainted wine. The Psalmist described the verbal and physical abuse Jesus would suffer and even foretold the soldiers' petty gambling for Jesus' clothes [Psalm 22:16-18]. Mark [15:29-32] portrayed a clear and horrible picture of the shouting and violence and Matthew, likely in tearful disgust, wrote of the shameless role of the dice [27:35, 36]. Yet despite all these horrible events, the Psalmist was able to end on a note of victory, assuring us that everyone from around the globe will worship the Lord, concluding with this declaration: *"His righteous acts will be told to those not yet born. They will hear about everything he has done"* [22:31].

We who know His salvation rejoice in these words; we who have read and believed Philippians 2: 10 know *"that at the name of Jesus every knee should bow, in heaven and on earth and under the earth"*; and like Isaiah we who have felt the call of God upon our hearts to preach the gospel know that *"the Good News must first be preached to all the nations"* [Mark 13:10] whether or not they will listen.

What are we to do with the miraculous fulfillment of the Old Testament prophecies? The evidence of Jesus' immeasurable love is written in every line, as is His willingness to give His life for ours. We can answer when He calls us and go where He directs. 'Here I am Lord, send me!'

I am He

It isn't just the prophecies that His crucifixion and resurrection fulfilled, it's also the miracles that took place during these events, the *"many infallible proofs"* – proofs that will not fail even under close examination. The miracles associated with the crucifixion begin in the Garden of Gethsemane.

There we find Jesus sweating drops of blood. Doctor Luke described the event in Luke 22:43-44. This referenced a rare medical condition called haematohidrosis. Under great emotional stress, the blood vessels around the sweat glands constrict and if the trauma is severe enough the vessels rupture. Blood is then mixed with the sweat and is pushed to the surface, appearing as droplets of blood mixed with sweat. Jesus' physical response identified His anguish over His upcoming suffering and crucifixion. He knew that the unity that He and the Father had shared for countless ages would be severed when He took upon Himself the sins for all humankind. His perfect and holy Father could not look upon Him as He was covered in our sin, thus Jesus cried out, both in fulfillment of prophecy and personal torment at being separated from His heavenly Father: *"My God, my God, why have you abandoned me?"* [Matthew 27:46]

The next miracle we see is the arresting soldiers' response to Jesus when He questioned them in the Garden of Gethsemane. Jesus knew His hour had come and His arrest was imminent. Courageously He stepped forward, asking them to state their business, and when they did, calmly replied: "*I AM* he," [John 18:5]. Yet when He declared Himself with the ancient identification "*I AM*", those who had come for Him, fell to the ground. Did you read that – they fell to the ground!

Then a fight broke out and in his wasted zeal, Peter sliced off the ear of the high priest's servant, Malchus, but Jesus reached out and with a hand that would soon be stained with His own blood, healed the wound. Facing arrest and torture, knowing the brutality that was yet to come, Jesus took a moment to extend healing to someone who was hurting. He took the time to heal the wounds of one of His enemies. Can you imagine the utter amazement of everyone present? Right before their eyes, blood still dripping through Malchus' fingers where he had grabbed his gushing wound, all could see his ear was restored. Not a scratch on him. They must have gaped in amazement. But Jesus took hold of the moment once again, quietly asking that His men not be arrested, fulfilling the prophecy that none would be taken [John 18:8-9; John 6:39]. As He did for Malchus and His disciples, so He does for us; He intercedes to ensure the safety of His loved ones.

After enduring the cruel lashes of the whip, the battering of the crown of thorns on His scalp, and the brazen mockery of the soldiers and rejection of Peter, Jesus still had to face an incensed crowd screaming for His death. Then, exhausted beyond human capacity, Jesus was forced to carry His cross on His bruised and bleeding body. The weight of the entire cross is believed to have been about 300 pounds and if he only carried the horizontal bar, the patibulum, it would have weighed between 75 and 125 pounds. By the time that the crossbar was thrust upon shoulders, He'd already been awake all night, endured a brutal beating and the knife-like crown of thorns had pierced His head. With the pain, loss of blood and lack of sleep, Jesus was so weak that He stumbled as He made his way up the Via Dolorosa, a walk of almost three miles from his flogging to the site of His crucifixion. The fact that He made the journey at all is a miracle, and no wonder He stumbled. When that happened, Simon was then recruited to carry Christ's cross the rest of the way to the Skull.

Upon arrival, He was thrown to the ground and huge nails

estimated to be 5 – 9 inches long were pounded through his wrists and feet. Thus, in order to breathe He had to lift Himself by His feet in order to fill His lungs with oxygen. Even during such agony, He thought of those around Him. When the criminal hanging beside Him defended His innocence and requested that Jesus remember him when He received His kingdom, Jesus welcomed him to paradise [Luke 23:39-43].

Similarly, when He looked down upon His grieving mother, He comforted her with the only words He could offer, giving her into the care of the disciple whom He loved [John 19:26,27]. These passages alone should reassure us that Jesus is always keenly aware of our needs and makes spiritual, emotional and physical provision for us.

When Jesus gasped his last breath, uttering *"Father, forgive them for they don't know what they are doing"* [Luke 23:34] He offers us the example of forgiveness to even our worst enemy. With the dimming of the Light of the world, the sun's brilliance was also covered [Mark 15:33], and at His death the thunderclap of heaven and earth resounded, signally to those who would listen that Jesus had finished His earthly mission [John 19:30].

As Jesus surrendered His Spirit, the temple curtain was ripped from top to bottom opening the Holy of Holies, enabling all to enter into God's presence [Matthew 27:50-52]. Still the earth groaned, rumbling in agony and opening graves to release the dead to life. We do not know what happened to these resurrected people. If it was just a momentary revelation of their physical restoration, or if, like Lazarus, they lived for many years more. What is important is that as Jesus proclaimed, by His death, life will spring forth [John 12:23-26].

An earthquake occurred a second time pushing aside the stone covering the tomb which had harbored Jesus's body, sending the soldiers in spasms of fear [Matthew 28:2-4]. Bible scholars have estimated that the stone would have weighed almost two tons. Only brute force and the combined effort of many men could have moved such an obstacle, yet it was the finger of God which shook the earth and plucked the stone out of the way of His Son. It was done not to free Jesus from the tomb, but to reveal to the world that He had, in fact, already escaped.

When the women arrived to care for Jesus' body, they were greeted by angels who reassured them that Jesus lives [Matthew 28:5-7]. Still today, Jesus seeks to turn our mourning into joy and our despair into purpose as He did for the women who visited His tomb. He personally addressed Mary, revealing His resurrection and commissioning her to take a message to His "brothers" [John 20:11-18]. Likewise with us, Jesus sees our grief and as only He can, comes to each of us in our darkest moments to reassure us of His living presence and remind us that our lives are still filled with purpose just as Jeremiah wrote in 29:11-14.

Jesus appeared as well to His grieving friends as they returned to their village in Emmaus. Luke wrote of this remarkable account in chapter 24. Downhearted, the two men were dragging their feet homeward when an apparent stranger walked up beside them and asked them what they were talking about. Not recognizing their new companion, they explained that the Messiah they'd hoped would free them from enslavement had been killed. They even reported the astounding news from the women who proclaimed He now lived. Seeing their confusion and despair, Jesus patiently recounted the Scriptures which foretold these very events, and when invited into their home for a meal, broke bread before them, then vanished. Can you imagine their astonishment? So too with us. We may not always recognize the message or messenger that God brings, but when we have ears to hear, and hearts to respond, we will discover life-giving truths and receive hope in hopeless situations.

In the same way He visited His disciples; even locked doors could not keep Him out. In every instance, His message was always the same: "*Peace be with you*". In those moments, He revealed the nature and reality of His resurrection, released the promised Holy Spirit, and instructed them to transmit His message of forgiveness to the world [John 20:19-31].

Finally, it is the miraculous transformation of His disciples from fearful fishermen to courageous evangelists. We see it in Peter who was trembling with such great fear that he couldn't face the accusations of women around a campfire. Then, empowered by the Holy Spirit, he became an influential messenger who would face down the high priests and even death itself to bring the supernatural news of Jesus' death and resurrection.

The same transformation is possible for us when we surrender to the hand of God and are filled with the Holy Spirit. Through Jesus' death and resurrection, we are given the gift of eternal life. Whatever we were in the past, we can be more, more than we could have imagined or hoped. This is the miracle of the Cross and Rebirth.

Our God reigns

In the life and even in the death of Jesus, miracles abound. It is simply a part of everything He is and does. By His crucifixion, Jesus fulfills the prophecies foretold by Isaiah in chapter 53 and David in Psalm 22. These prophecies predicted that Jesus would be rejected, beaten, nailed, and speared; they also promised that His back would be raked by the lash of a whip and His garments surrendered to the role of the dice. With His resurrection we see that Jesus fulfilled David's prediction that His body would not remain in the grave [Psalm 16:10], just as He would accomplish the liberation of those captured by sin as Isaiah foretold [61:1].

Equally miraculous are the events surrounding His ascension when He returned to His heavenly Father. In Luke 24, He reminded His disciples what He'd been telling them throughout His three years with them. *"When I was with you before, I told you that everything written about me in the law of Moses and the prophets and in the Psalms must be fulfilled." Then he opened their minds to understand the Scriptures."* [Luke 24:44,45]

He wanted them - and us - to understand that what occurred when He was arrested in the Garden, when His back was flailed with the cat- of- nine -tails, and then when He was forced to carry His cross through the Via Dolorosa was all part of God's plan. Even when His journey ended with nails pounded into His hands and feet, He was fulfilling God's promise. Each word He uttered offered confirmation and comfort of who He was, the Savior of the world.

But the grave wasn't His end. He may have foretold His suffering and death, but He always vowed He would rise again. The grave was not His home, heaven was. The event is described in Mark 16, Luke 24 and Acts 1. *"Then Jesus led them to Bethany, and lifting his hands to heaven, he blessed them. While he was blessing them, he left them and was taken up to heaven."* [Luke 24:50-51]. There is no mention of a fiery chariot that transported Elijah to heaven, just a marvelous and miraculous elevation until He was out of their sight. But the disciples were not daunted that they could see their Master no longer. He had commissioned them in Mark 16 to travel everywhere teaching, baptizing, and performing miracles through the Holy Spirit's power. And so they did.

These events transformed the timid disciples into mighty men of faith and valor. Through their work the gospel spread across the Middle East, Europe and beyond. These unsophisticated, uneducated men no longer hid in fear or returned to the mundane task of casting nets for fish. They went forth boldly becoming fishers of men.

Why were these men so galvanized? Because they believed His parting promise: *"Be sure of this: I am with you always, even to the end of the age."* [Matthew 28:20]. Their hearts resonated with God's words recorded by the prophet Isaiah: *"Don't be afraid, for I am with you. Don't be discouraged, for I am your God. I will strengthen you and help you. I will hold you up with my victorious right hand."* [Isaiah 41:10] Not only this but He promised them He'd return to take them home [John 14:2,3].

These promises are our promises, spoken to us His twenty-first century children with the same conviction as those given to His disciples in the first century. These are the guarantees given at His ascension. They are redeeming, empowering, emboldening. And so we, too, can rise on eagles' wings, and run and not grow weary and walk and not faint [Isaiah 40:31].

The Miracle of Pentecost

We have by no means exhausted the miracles of the gospels, but today we are going to look at the opening miracle recorded in the book of Acts: The Miracle of Pentecost. For the Jews, Pentecost refers to the celebration of Shavuot occurring on the sixth of Sivan depending on the year in the Jewish calendar. It is a festival celebrating the first fruits of the harvest as described in Leviticus 23. According to the law of Moses, the harvest offering was first presented at the end of Passover and again seven weeks later. Thus, the Feast of Weeks, or the Feast of the Harvest [Exodus 23:16] was the time to give the second holy offering [Numbers 28:26]. As this celebration was held fifty days after Passover, for the New Testament believers it was known in Greek as Pentecost, meaning fiftieth, and became synonymous with the outpouring of the Holy Spirit and the first harvest of post resurrection believers.

Jesus had instructed the disciples to wait in Jerusalem for the Holy Spirit to come and fill them with power [Luke 24:49]. Luke emphasized this event when he sent his friend Theophilus his second letter, explaining in Acts 1:8 that the Father promised to send them His special gift. Can you imagine your own excitement at this news? Your Teacher, who had exceeded all your expectations, fulfilled every promise, performed amazing miracles, taught incredible truths, even rose from the dead, was sending you His Holy Spirit. Of course, you would wait for it. And they did and this is what happened: "*Suddenly,*

*there was a sound from heaven like the roaring of a mighty windstorm, and
it filled the house where they were sitting. Then, what looked like flames or
tongues of fire appeared and settled on each of them. And everyone present
was filled with the Holy Spirit and began speaking in other languages, as
the Holy Spirit gave them this ability."* [Acts 2:2-4]

A mighty, roaring wind, and flames of fire. Both are cleansing
elements – the wind blowing away all the dust and dirt and the fire
burning away any impurities as Numbers 31:23 explains. The prophet
Malachi speaks of the same cleansing process [3:3] as does the prophet
Zechariah in 13:9. God was bringing the disciples to a whole new level
of maturity and ministry. He was taking them from their face-to-face
instruction by Jesus to the internal guidance of the Holy Spirit.

Not only were they filled with power, but they were given a gift
of languages. Luke explains that there were Jews from all over the vast
region who had come to Jerusalem to celebrate the Feast of the Harvest.
Mosaic law dictated that this celebration was one of the three Jewish
holidays in which the entire male population came together to worship
the Lord [Deuteronomy 16:16]. Thus, devout Jews from miles around
were present for this miraculous event.

Moreover, even though they came from different areas and spoke
diverse languages, God ensured that there would be no confusion or
misunderstanding. He empowered the words of the disciples to be
heard in the people's many dialects [Acts 2:5-12]. In that moment,
God superseded any potential human impediment by enabling each
person present to hear the gospel message in his or her own language.
It was truly a complete and miraculous reversal of what occurred at the
Tower of Babel [Genesis 11] when God separated humanity by creating
different languages. Here God was bringing them to Himself and
erasing their confusion by ensuring that they could hear the message
of salvation in their own tongue.

Yet for some, doubts remained and they mocked what they heard.
How sad to think that some hear and see a miracle and then mock
its power or source. Fortunately, many others listened spell bound as
Peter spoke. Knowing he had primarily a Jewish audience before him,
he took them to the prophet Joel who foretold this event when God

would out His Spirit upon all people [Joel 2:28-32]. Then Peter fast forwarded them to the life of Jesus, explaining: *"God publicly endorsed Jesus the Nazarene by doing powerful miracles, wonders, and signs through him, as you well know."* [Acts 2:22]. Remember that it had only been fifty days since the crucifixion of Jesus Christ, and all the miracles and teachings that Jesus had done during His three active years of ministry had undoubtedly reached them, even the knowledge of His death by crucifixion. But what they probably didn't know or believe was His resurrection and thus Peter told them of this miracle and how it had occurred: *"God released him from the horrors of death and raised him back to life, for death could not keep him in its grip".* [Acts 2:24]

It's possible, if not likely, they'd heard the tale told by the Jewish leaders that Jesus' body had been stolen from the tomb, and He hadn't in fact rose from the dead. Peter wanted to discredit this account and spread the truth that Jesus had risen from the grave. We can almost see his eyes ablaze with conviction and his stance tall, back straight, hands gesturing with firm sweeps to emphasize his words: *"God raised Jesus from the dead, and we are all witnesses of this."* [Acts 2:32] Peter seems to be saying: 'You tried to end His life, silence His words, stop His miracles, but it could not be. So use your words not for carrying tales, but telling the truth. Tell everyone this magnificent story' [Acts 2:36].

How did his listeners respond? Luke tells us that their hearts were pierced. They were struck to the core with the power of Peter's words. They knew them to be truth and they knew their sins had placed Jesus on that cross. They felt the ache of conviction, and they cried out for direction. Peter didn't hesitate in answering: *"Each of you must **repent** of your sins and **turn** to God, and be **baptized** in the name of Jesus Christ for the forgiveness of your sins. Then you **will receive** the gift of the Holy Spirit. This promise is to you, to your children, and even to the Gentiles - all who have been called by the Lord our God."* [Acts 2:38] Four specific actions are required: **Repent** – turn from your sins; **Turn** – go to God; **Baptize** – publicly submerge in water to show inner cleansing; **Receive** – open your hearts to the Holy Spirit.

What an absolutely miraculous day! And it can be your day, too. Wherever you are, whatever you've done, you can know forgiveness, you can know restoration, you can have a relationship with God. Seek Him, ask Him to forgive you. Request your pastor to baptize you and request the Holy Spirit to fill you. It can be a new day for you, too. Experience your own Pentecost today.

The Lame Beggar

Thinking about miracles often takes us just through the gospels of Matthew, Mark, Luke and John, the direct works of Jesus during His earthly ministry. Yet a look at the book of Acts shows us that the miracles didn't end when Jesus ascended to heaven. The New Testament church and its members continued to fulfill God's healing plan of hope in the world. And it started right away.

In the second chapter we read about the presence and power of the Holy Spirit radically transforming the disciples from frightened fishermen to bold evangelists. Jesus had promised them the Holy Spirit and with His power they'd proclaim Jesus everywhere [Acts 1:8]. We often imagine that to witness for Jesus we must tell others about Him, yet in studying the gospels, we learn that Jesus witnessed of the goodness and mercy of God by His miraculous acts as much as by His teaching. In fact, it was His miracles of healing that caused the multitudes to leave their homes and rush to wherever He was [Matthew 14:13,14].

Miracles get people's attention and that is what we see in reading Acts 2. The mighty rushing wind and tongues of fire have visited Peter, John and the other disciples and 3000 came to faith from their powerful message. But unlike earlier, the disciples didn't return to fishing; they didn't go back to their old life. Instead they worshipped regularly in the Temple. It was during one such visit that they noticed an invalid seated by the entrance. And it's here that our story gets interesting.

Not only were Peter and John seeking God through prayer, but they were searching for ways to serve Him. Perhaps they'd seen this man during other temple visits. They may have even observed his family carrying him to the place by this Beautiful Gate. Certainly, they knew that this man, unable to assist the family through manual labor, hoped to aid his loved ones through the small bits of coin that came his way through a compassionate worshipper. In fact, he was used to people's generosity and when Peter spoke to him directly, he held out his hand, awaiting the expected token. But God and Peter had other plans. Their solution wasn't momentary but monumental. Life changing. *"I don't have any silver or gold for you. But I'll give you what I have. In the name of Jesus Christ the Nazarene, get up and walk!"* [Acts 3:6] You can almost hear the vibrancy in this declaration. *"In the name of Jesus Christ the Nazarene, get up and walk!"*

What happened next? *"Then Peter took the lame man by the right hand and helped him up. And as he did, the man's feet and ankles were instantly healed and strengthened. He jumped up, stood on his feet, and began to walk! Then, walking, leaping, and praising God, he went into the Temple with them."* [Acts 3:7,8] The transformation in this man was instantaneous. Shriveled limbs grew muscles, twisted bones became straightened. Yet it wasn't just his body that was healed, but his heart as well. His gratitude to God was immediate with shouts of praise, and like King David, an exuberant dance. Moreover, the first place he headed was into the Temple.

I love this part of the story. How many of us experience a miracle and then go on with our lives as if nothing happened? We don't tell others what God did and we don't go to church to sing His praises. I truly hope that anyone reading this who has experienced God's divine intervention has faithfully praised God for His amazing works. Just recently a lady came to me and said, 'do you remember texting me with words of encouragement. It came just at the right time when I was ready to break down and cry. Your message told me God loved me and cared about me. The miraculous timing spoke to my heart and to this day I remember it. Every time I am in the city, I visit your church. Moreover, I want to be able to help others. Just tell me what I can do.'

She responded just like the man in our story. God healed her broken heart and she praised Him, worshipped in His house and sought ways to give to others.

What's so wonderful about the man in Acts 3 is that he wasn't the only one affected by this miracle. Everyone who knew of his paralysis could see he was healed. They couldn't doubt the evidence of a miracle [Acts 3:9-11] and witnessing this event made their hearts ready for the gospel and when Peter told them about Jesus Christ, 2,000 more believed [Acts 4:4].

Yet the Temple leaders and guards refused to receive the message and arrested Peter and John, tossing them into jail for the night. The next morning, they were dragged before the Council and the same men who'd condemned Jesus to death now interrogated them. Peter and John weren't alarmed. After all Jesus had prepared His disciples for this moment and assured them they'd know what to say [Like 12:11,12]. Boldly Peter proclaimed the message of the cross and the power of the resurrection [Acts 4:8-11], stating: *"There is salvation in no one else! God has given no other name under heaven by which we must be saved."* [Acts 4:12]

The Council was speechless. Two unlearned men, mere fishermen, spoke with the same authority and confidence they'd heard Jesus use. Moreover, there before them was the man who'd been healed. He too was standing tall, face radiant with joy. Caiaphas and his cronies raged. The miracles hadn't stopped with Jesus' death. What were they to do? 'Keep quiet', they ordered, but Peter and John were unfazed. They'd seen the resurrected Lord; they'd felt the fire from the Holy Spirit burn through them. How could they ever keep silent? They would never deny the Lord again.

What about you? What are you saying about the miracles Christ has done in your life? Are others amazed when they hear your testimony? Do you have people telling you to keep quiet? Do you stand in the power of Jesus' name, boldly proclaiming what Christ has done? If you do, it's likely that you, too, will soon be living the book of Acts.

A Miraculous Journey

We don't often think of Olympic class feats occurring in the New Testament. We may recall the Old Testament account of Samson's amazing weight lifting achievements when he pushed down the pillars of Dagon's temple in Gaza [Judges 16] and his other incredible exploits, but otherwise we don't witness too many achievements of that nature. There are many more of a different sort that we will look at later in this book, but today, however, we are going to see a miracle reminiscent of Elijah's amazing race against Ahab's chariot [1 Kings 18].

Following the explosion of believers with the preaching of Peter and the other disciples, including the miracle of the lame man at the temple [Acts 3], the early church members were meeting together and sharing generously with one another as Acts 2:42-47 explains. Yet not everyone wanted to participate that generously, as we see in the story of Ananias and Sapphira in Acts 5. Although there was no requirement to give, the couple wanted to give the appearance of spirituality and humility while in fact they were anything but. Of course, if you've read that chapter, you know that when questioned each said they'd sold the field for the price they'd specified, but the Holy Spirit knew their deception and for it, He literally took their breath away. This tragic miracle convinced the believers not to mess around with false piety or generosity.

Yet the many signs and wonders performed by the apostles

continued to attract people to the message of the gospel and, just as when Jesus ministered throughout the region, people were once again carrying their sick into the streets, hoping that even Peter's shadow would fall on them. We read that even those from the surrounding areas were bringing their physically, mentally and emotionally sick relatives and all were healed [Acts 5:16].

The Sadducees, again enraged by the miraculous works of God, threw the apostles in jail. But bars or guards couldn't stop the work of God and the cell gates were miraculously opened [Acts 5:19]. In fact, the book of Acts records three different instances were an angel opens prison doors, freeing the apostles so they could continue preaching. We'll be looking more closely at these miracles when we read further on in Acts 12 with Peter and Acts 16 with Paul and Silas.

But today's study looks at Philip the Evangelist. Although some commentaries may separate him from the Philip that Jesus selects as a disciple [John 1:43] who comes from Bethsaida, Andrew and Peter's hometown, I am inclined to think they are one and the same. This Philip gave his testimony to Nathaniel proclaiming Jesus as the One that Moses foretold. He is also the Philip who brought the little boy's lunch to Jesus [John 6:5-6] to initiate the miraculous feeding of the 5,000. Yet he also questions Jesus, asking Him to show them the Father [John 14:8-11] and Jesus reassures him that if he has seen Him, he has seen the Father. Philip, then, remains faithful through the crucifixion and resurrection and is present when Jesus ascends to heaven [Acts 1:13-15] as well as the outpouring of the Holy Spirit described in Acts 2. In Acts 6, he is selected along with Stephen and five others to distribute food to the widows. However, the persecutions drive him from Jerusalem to Samaria to preach the gospel were his message of Christ was eagerly received and many were healed through his ministry [Acts 8]. One amongst the crowd was Simon, a sorcerer, was also doing impressive acts earning him the moniker "The Great One – the Power of God" [Acts 8:10]. Yet even he believed Philip's message and was baptized, following him everywhere.

Then Philip received new instructions: *"Go south down the desert road that runs from Jerusalem to Gaza. So he started out, and he met the treasurer of Ethiopia, a eunuch of great authority under the Kandake, the* *queen of Ethiopia. The eunuch had gone to Jerusalem to worship, and he* *was now returning. Seated in his carriage, he was reading aloud from the* *book of the prophet Isaiah. The Holy Spirit said to Philip, "Go over and* *walk along beside the carriage.""* [Acts 8:26-29]

The instructions were specific: where to go, who to seek and what to do. The Holy Spirit had prepared Philip, teaching him so he could teach others. Then following the instruction that Jesus gave them in Matthew 28:19 to make disciples and baptize, Philip taught the Ethiopian the meaning of the passage in Isaiah, explaining in such a compelling manner how it was fulfilled in the life of Jesus Christ. Eagerly, the eunuch asked to be baptized and once it was accomplished, Philip disappeared from his sight [Acts 8:36-40]. This confirmed the power of the gospel and the eunuch praised God for what he'd seen and heard, while Philip was transported to another town, Azotus, to continue preaching about Jesus.

Miraculously Philip found the one man on this desert road who was reading a specific passage of Scripture that foretold the coming of Jesus Christ. The second miracle was that Philip was able to run up to a moving chariot and offer his pastoral services to a very wealthy man. That's an impressive Olympian feat. Moreover, the Ethiopian eunuch, clearly a man with a high position in the Queen's court, agreed to be instructed by this man who was simply jogging on the road beside him. Philip had no fancy chariot, no fancy clothes, was a complete stranger, yet the eunuch asked him to explain a difficult prophetic passage of scripture to him. Philip clearly wasn't a member of the Sanhedrin. He wasn't a Pharisee and he certainly didn't share the same wealth or status as the eunuch. Nonetheless the eunuch trusted Philip enough to welcome him into his chariot and receive his instruction. The next miracle was the eunuch's receptive faith to the message Philip offered concerning the good news of Jesus Christ, and he couldn't wait to be baptized.

What happens next is our fifth miracle. The Holy Spirit instantaneously transported Philip to Azotus, a city about twenty miles away from their current location and there Philip continued to preach the word of God. In Acts 21 we find him settled in Caesarea, having raised four daughters, each with prophetic gifts of their own. As for the eunuch, his conversion unfolded amazing events. He was the first published conversion of an African man, a man obviously seeking to understand the word of God, although not a Jew himself. It was likely that he was socially and religiously marginalized by his state as a eunuch, yet he nonetheless was earnest to have a relationship with God. Later church reports indicated that this eunuch took the message of salvation back to Ethiopia and, because of his testimony and preaching, a church was started there, resulting in the gospel reaching far beyond the borders of Jerusalem and Galilee.

This story clearly demonstrates that Christ reaches out to all people regardless of their status, state, religion or ethnic background. Furthermore, this story illustrates to us that lack of resources should never limit our willingness to preach the word of God. The Holy Spirit can arrange any manner of miracles to enable us to be evangelists and teachers of the Word – whether to someone on a desert Gaza road or sitting at a desk across from us at work. Jesus accomplishes the miraculous to ensure that those who seek Him will find Him when they search for Him with all their heart [Jeremiah 29:13].

Paul's New Life

We don't often attribute the book of Acts to miracles, but in fact it is filled with amazing incidents of the supernatural. Chapter 9 opens with the story of Saul who, enraged by the persistent teaching and miracles of the early church leaders, pursued their destruction. He even participated in the stoning of Stephen, despite having heard his profound message and witnessing his face aglow with the presence of God. In fact, Saul's heart had so hardened that he requested permission to capture and incarcerate more Christians in Damascus.

If you've read the story, you know that God had other plans for this tormented religious zealot. Light blasted from heaven and knocked him to the ground. Blinded by its brilliance, he hung his head in the dirt. A voice, clear and firm spoke into his stunned mind: *"Saul! Saul! Why are you persecuting me?"* [Acts 9:4] This was unexpected. This righteous Pharisee thought he was doing God's will so who could be speaking to him about persecution. *"Who are you, lord?" Saul asked. And the voice replied, "I am Jesus, the one you are persecuting!* [Acts 9:5]

How amazing would this be? The very one you sought to discredit, you believed to be blasphemously worshipped, the one you felt certain was dead and buried, was accusing you of wrongdoing. Not only that but He was issuing an order to you: *"Now get up and go into the city, and you will be told what you must do"* [Acts 9:6] and you felt compelled to obey. Physically sightless and spiritually astounded by the encounter,

Saul allowed himself to be led to Damascus where he remained blind and bewildered for three days. Then Ananias received the dubious instruction to go and pray for Saul of Tarsus, the Christian killer [Acts 9:11].

Disconcerted by the instruction, Ananias reminded God of Saul's reputation. What was God thinking to send him there? Have we ever questioned God's instruction, wondering if God has forgotten some important details that make His request impossible or dangerous to fulfill? 'But Lord', we say, only to have God answer as He did to Ananias with specific directions to the street, the home and the person he was to pray for. Despite his misgivings, Ananias obeyed and prayed for Saul. In turn Saul was instantly healed, baptized and set upon a journey that would impact the entire region. In his life Saul would travel over 10,000 miles, preaching the word of God to Jew and Gentile alike. Throughout his ministry, the hunter became the hunted and from place to place, city to city Jews sought to take his life. Yet with the same zeal that he set out to destroy the Christians, Saul, now Paul, set out to bring the life-giving message of salvation and new churches sprang up wherever he went.

What about you? From Paul's story, we can see it doesn't matter what we've done. When we accept Jesus Christ, our life story immediately changes and we become who we were meant to be. We can set aside our past and not dwell on our mistakes. We can remember the power of our testimony and recall the moment when Jesus became real in our lives and set our feet upon a new path of freedom for ourselves and others. Thus, we can't keep this great news to ourselves. As God did for Saul, He has done for us, miraculously delivering us from darkness to light, and we, too, can *"live a life filled with love, following the example of Christ."* [Ephesians 5:2].

Dorcas Lives Again

From the incredible story of Saul, the book of Acts moves to the miracles of Peter. Like Philip, Peter was sent by the Holy Spirit to evangelize and disciple new believers living outside of Jerusalem. In Acts 9 we find him in Lydda, a city that was twenty-five miles northwest of Jerusalem. Here he discovered new converts to Christianity, perhaps by the earlier ministry of Philip or even as a result of witnessing the miracle of Pentecost.

It is in this city that Peter was introduced to Aeneas who had been paralyzed for eight years. Following the example Christ set when He healed the paralyzed man lowered through the roof by his friends in Luke 5:18-26, Peter said to Aeneas: *"Jesus Christ heals you! Get up, and roll up your sleeping mat!"* [Acts 9:34] and Aeneas, like the man from the temple gate in Acts 3 was instantly healed.

In both instances, their immobile position was replaced with mobility and their weakness with strength? Even the very thing on which they reclined, a clear sign of their paralysis, was now tucked under their arm, a relic of their past, and their strong limbs were a testimony of this new life. In fact, when the people in that region saw this man, standing tall and walking with firm, athletic strides, they knew that God had performed a miracle. Their doubts were turned to faith, their skepticism to belief, and all in that region came to the Lord.

Twelve miles away in the seaport city of Joppa, there was a faithful woman of God whose Jewish name was Tabitha. Dorcas, her Greek name, means "gazelle", signifying her grace and beauty. The attribution of a Greek name as well as a Jewish name suggests that she was a Hellenist, someone who lives among the Greeks and speaks their language. However, it was also evident that she was a follower of Christ and an active member of the Joppa church. The original Greek version of this story titles her as a "mathetria" which means female disciple, and she was the only woman in the New Testament to be given such a distinctive and respectful title, suggesting that she was highly regarded for her faith and charitable works. As a result, when she became ill and died, many in the region mourned her passing. While some were preparing her for burial, surprisingly others had other ideas. They were not contemplating death, but life.

Having heard that Peter was only twelve miles away, less than a day's journey, and was performing healing miracles there, they decided to go to him and ask him to pray for their dear friend Dorcas. Now we aren't told if they had actually told him that she had died, but whatever their specific request, Peter accompanied them back to Joppa and found that Dorcas' body had been laid in the home's upper room. Few of us can hear the words "Upper Room" without thinking of Acts 2 and the Pentecost miracle when the Holy Spirit came with incredible force and indwelt the believers worshipping in that holy place. Perhaps Peter, also remembered the Jerusalem Upper Room and trusted God would show Himself just as powerfully.

Yet, all around him were weeping widows. That must have been distracting and disturbing. Dorcas obviously had many friends and her death had greatly affected them and left them grief-stricken. As if wanting to prove how wonderful Dorcas had been, they showed Peter the many garments she'd made for the needy in their area and recounted the numerous stories of her generosity. The commotion was probably similar to what Jesus faced with the mourners at Jairus' home in Mark 5:40. It was unlikely anyone was expecting a miracle. Thus, gently, but firmly Peter had to usher the mourners out of the room. He needed a quiet place, a place to settle his mind and thoughts on the possibilities of restoration and not the actuality of death. Once he was spiritually in tune with what the Holy Spirit wanted, he turned to the body of Dorcas and said just as Jesus did to Jairus' daughter: *"Get up Tabitha!"* [Acts 9:40].

Immediately *"she opened her eyes! When she saw Peter, she sat up!"* There is no discussion of what she was or where she had been. Peter simply reached out his hand to her and helped her to her feet. Tabitha was fully restored and whatever illness had taken her life was completely gone from her body. No doubt she was a little surprised to see a man in her room and realized that she was dressed for a funeral and not a church service, but I'm sure that Peter quickly explained what had happened. He no doubt also knew the prayerful anticipation of those just outside the door and he called Tabitha's friends to come in and greet their dear one who was now very much alive.

Can you imagine the buzz of excitement that must have spread through that house, out the door, into the street, spreading like wild fire as it passed from mouth to mouth? The widows who had washed her body were likely holding her hand and stroking her face in absolute wonder at this living proof of God's power. Similarly, the men who'd gone to retrieve Peter must have been equally amazed. Perhaps the widows didn't even know why the men went to fetch Peter, for when they had returned, tears were still streaming down the women's faces and their hands were still clutching the garments she had sown. But these men hoped, they believed, they knew what God could do and trusted that their beloved friend would not yet rest in the ground.

When the townspeople learned of the miracle, many came to faith in Christ. Once again, the impact of God doing the impossible brought about an amazing harvest of souls. In fact, we are told that Peter remained in Joppa for some time to ensure the growth of this new church. This chapter in Acts relates amazing miracles: from Saul's conversion, to Aeneas' healing to Dorcas's return from the dead.

As people of the Spirit, we should be encouraged by the evidence of our Savior's power actualized through His disciples. Philippians 2:13

states: *"For God is working in us, giving us the desire and the power to do what pleases Him."* With His Spirit living in us, we are always equipped to participate in His glorious plan of salvation and healing. Every day is a great day with Him.

All are Welcome

In the book of Acts, we see that miracles are not always limited to physical or psychological healing. The definition of a miracle, we recall, is an extraordinary event which occurs only through divine intervention, an overt action of God which transforms a situation or a person. This is what occurs when Cornelius meets God or perhaps I should say when God meets Cornelius as told in Acts 10. Cornelius was a god-fearing Roman officer who held the prestigious position of centurion, which in our terms means that he was a captain of an Italian regiment. Although not a Jew himself, he had come to accept the God of Israel and in his devotion *"gave generously to the poor and prayed regularly to God"* [Acts 10:2].

His faith had clearly caught the attention of both the Jews and God for we are told: *"One afternoon about three o'clock, he had a vision in which he saw an angel of God coming toward him"* and calling him by name [Acts 10:3]. As any of us can imagine, Cornelius was stunned at the sight and fearful of what this visitation might mean. Imagine his even greater amazement when the angel said: *"Your prayers and gifts to the poor have been received by God as an offering! Now send men to Joppa, and summon a man named Simon Peter."* [Acts 10:4,5]

That is like hearing 'God has noticed all that you've been doing for Him and others.' Isn't that what all of us want to hear, the *Well done, thou good and faithful servant* that Jesus speaks about [Matthew

25:23 KJV]. Well this was Cornelius's well done. And he didn't waste any time responding to the directive. Immediately he called his staff and sent some of them off to Joppa to find Peter. You may recall from Acts 9 that Peter was evangelizing in that region following the incredible restoration of Dorcas, but would Peter be ready for these Gentile messengers. Up until this point Peter had only witnessed and ministered to the Jews. He had seen the Holy Spirit fill the Jewish believers in Jerusalem at Pentecost in Acts 2; been used by God to heal the lame man seated outside the temple in Acts 3 and participated in the healing of Aeneas in Lydda and Dorcas in Joppa in Acts 9. Except for Philip's teaching to the Ethiopian eunuch (Acts 8), the entire ministry of the disciples and the baptism by the Holy Spirit had been to Jews.

The disciples clearly had the idea that Jesus' message of salvation was only to be delivered to and received by the Children of Israel. After all didn't He say to the Syro-Phoenician mother that he *was sent only to help God's lost sheep – the people of Israel*" [Matthew 15:24]. Perhaps they'd forgotten that Jesus was so delighted at her humble, faith-filled answer that He'd applauded her faith and healed her daughter. It's possible that they failed to remember His universal directive in Matthew 28:19 to preach to people of all nations.

But just in case, Peter didn't understand, before Cornelius' staff arrived, God gave him a vision. He was up on the rooftop praying and began to feel his tummy grumbling with hunger when a sheet filled with animals a devout Jew should never eat was lowered before him. Then, to his astonishment, he was told to make a meal of them. This was a shocking sight for Peter and a horrific instruction. 'Was this a test?' Peter must have wondered. Was God trying to see if he was ruled by his belly and not by his faith. Peter stood firm. He refused to do it. But surprisingly that wasn't the answer God wanted and He repeated the vision and instructions three times to make sure Peter got the message: *"Do not call something unclean if God has made it clean."* [Acts 10:15]. Yet, despite the repetition, Peter was still uncertain how he was to interpret the vision. 'Does this mean I can eat anything now and no longer have to follow Jewish traditions?' It was only when Cornelius' men arrived that revelation came. *"Get up, go downstairs, and go with them without hesitation. Don't worry, for I have sent them."* [Acts 10:20]

Do you notice that the Holy Spirit didn't spell it out? He didn't say: 'the men who have come aren't Jewish, but you are to go with them anyway.' Still Peter wanted to be certain. He queried the men about why they came, and they explained that they were sent by a Roman officer named Cornelius, a god-fearing, faith-filled man. They went on to explain that an angel had instructed Cornelius to get Peter for he was to deliver a message of great importance. Peter was beginning to get the picture, and so the next day he went to Cornelius' house.

Cornelius was so overwhelmed that he fell at Peter's feet and tried to worship him. Fortunately, Peter wasn't puffed with pride by all that he'd seen, heard and done for Jesus. He pulled Cornelius up, declaring: *"Stand up! I'm a human being just like you!"* [Acts 10:26] This is a great reminder for all the mighty messengers of God who may perhaps imagine that they deserve special attention for all they do for Jesus. If Peter could walk with Jesus, receive the Holy Spirit through tongues of fire, heal the sick and raise the dead and still insist that others not bow before him, then surely there is no one in ministry today, no matter what they've accomplished, that should expect special treatment for their service. For whatever we do, it's still only accomplished by the gracious hand of God and we're all just human beings who should say with the psalmist: *"what are mere mortals that you should think about them, human beings that you should care for them?"* [Psalm 8:4]

When Peter went inside Cornelius' home and saw the large group of people already assembled and eagerly waiting to hear what he had to say, he couldn't help but recount what God was doing. *"But God has shown me that I should no longer think of anyone as impure or unclean. So I came without objection as soon as I was sent for."* [Acts 10:28,29]. Peter's response was an awesome indication that he understood clearly what God was doing: *"God shows no favoritism."* He explained: *In every nation he accepts those who fear him and do what is right. This is the message of Good News for the people of Israel—that there is peace with God through Jesus Christ, who is Lord of all."* [Acts 10:34,35]

Peter went on to explain the ministry of Jesus, His death and resurrection and His instruction to preach the Good News to everyone. This anointed message had an immediate effect within the hearts of Cornelius and his household. The Holy Spirit met them, filled them and they began to speak in other tongues and praise God. Peter then realized that not only did God intend for the Gentiles to receive salvation through Jesus Christ, but also the baptism of the Holy Spirit as well as water baptism. God wanted them to have the complete spiritual package.

But the early church leaders weren't completely convinced. News of the conversion of the Gentiles spread rapidly back to Jerusalem and when Peter returned, he met with sharp criticism from the Jewish believers [Acts 11:3]. Peter had to carefully explain to them the entire sequence of events, from his heavenly vision of unclean animals, to the prepared hearts of Cornelius and all his household and their infilling by the Holy Spirit [Acts 11:15-17].

"Who was I to stand in God's way?" Peter asked them [Acts 11:17] What a potent lesson for us all that when and how God chooses to move is not for us to question. He decides the results; we just have to be obedient. Fortunately, the Jewish leaders agreed [Acts 11:18]. Still it would take them a while to accept what God was doing. When Paul commenced his full-time ministry to the Gentiles [Acts 13:46] he received considerable condemnation. Even Peter vacillated and later stopped eating with the Gentiles, an action that Paul publicly rebuked [Galatians 2:11-21].

Where are we in all this today? Is everyone welcome to sit at our table, to sit beside us at church, to worship with us on Sundays and throughout the week? God would not have brought this message to us if He didn't know that we needed to experience the miracle of reconciliation on every level, receiving both His message of unity and equality as well as all those He welcomes to His eternal table. Let us be people of restoration and harmony that the gospel message can sing its pure, sweet notes in our lives.

Prison Doors Open

Miracles just keep happening in the book of Acts as we're going to see in Acts 12. It isn't physical healing or transport or even life restoration. This chapter shows us what freeing captives looks like in the New Testament church. As we've seen, preaching the gospel can be dangerous business. It can even cost you your life. James (John's brother) discovered this first hand. King Herod Agrippa, whose uncle, Herod Antipas, beheaded John the Baptist and participated in the trial of Jesus, was also a godless man who sought his own pleasure and defied God. He constantly curried favor with the ruling Romans and borrowed huge amounts of money to fund his lavish lifestyle and entertain his rich, influential friends. Once he became ruler in the region, he seemed to take an interest in pacifying the Jewish religious leaders. When Caligula, imagining himself a god, wanted to set up statues of himself even in the Holy of Holies, Herod Agrippa managed to talk him out of it. Thus, when he took it upon himself to attack the new sect of believers who followed the teachings of Jesus, he won the lasting admiration of the Pharisees and Sadducees. Hence, it was with great relish that he began executing Jewish believers, and had James executed by the sword. Determined to end the life of Peter in the same way, he had Peter thrown into prison, intending to present him for a very public trial after Passover. As if to illustrate the importance of Peter as a prisoner, he had him guarded by four squads of four soldiers each, somehow imagining that this simple fisherman could stage a jail break and escape his death sentence.

As we have repeatedly seen, it's impossible to thwart the plans of God. An angel visited the sleeping Peter, tapped his side, while the chains fell off his wrists. Then he ordered Peter to dress and follow him out of the cell. How would we feel the night before a major trial which decided if we'd live or die? It's doubtful we'd be sleeping. Even when I know I have an important event the next day or a weighty responsibility pressing on my shoulders, I find myself tossing and turning all night, thoughts of what is ahead always niggling at the back of my mind and prickling at the edge of my dreams. Yet Peter was far more composed. He knew his fellow believers were praying for him, but most importantly he knew that his life and his future was in God's hands. Whether he lived or died he would be with the Lord. And so he slept, even chain-linked between two soldiers. In fact, he slept so soundly that when a bright light filled his cramped, filthy cell he didn't awaken. Nor did he awaken when the angel stood before him. The angel had to jostle him awake. Now that's a peaceful sleep.

When Peter finally woke up, instantly the cruel chains that had bit into his thin wrists fell away. Slowly with the usual pins and needles of restored circulation, Peter moved his arms and legs again. Glancing at the sleeping guards, he saw that they didn't even stir when the chains clanked against the wall, when the angel called loudly or when he scrambled to dress. Their raspy snores continued to fill the room. 'Surely, I'm still asleep', thought Peter. 'Surely this is just a dream, showing me what I wish for, the freedom for which I and my friends have been praying. It can't really be happening – to me'. He looked about him in amazement as they passed the first and second guard posts. Then before them was an iron gate, but soundlessly, it unlatched itself and swung open. He was free. The prison was behind him, and the dark, empty street was ahead. He looked back one more time and watched the gate swing noiselessly closed. When he turned, his angelic companion was gone. He was alone in the street.

He reached out a tentative hand and felt the rock wall to the side of him. He stamped both feet on the cobbled lane and felt the firmness of earth beneath him. It was real. It was all real. An angel of the Lord had come for him, delivered him from armed guards, and led him to freedom. The hands of his enemy no longer imprisoned him. Those seeking his death had nothing but air. Euphoric with this knowledge, he dashed down the street. He had to tell his friends. Mary, he'd go to Mary's house, the mother of John Mark. They'd all gathered there to pray for him. Despite the lateness of the hour, he rapped firmly on the door. Rhoda, a young servant girl tentatively opened it and peered nervously around the edge of the door. Could it be the Roman guards or the temple soldiers? Each deadly group knew where they lived and were determined to destroy them. But no, it wasn't brawny men in uniforms with angry scowls upon their faces and sharp spears in their hands. It was Peter, his beard and hair long and straggly and his clothes creased and grey with dirt.

In a crazy combination of fear and joy, Rhoda slammed the door in his face and ran to tell the others inside the wonderful news. Of course, having prayed for hours for Peter's safe release, they received her news with jubilation. Not quite. They didn't believe her. *"You're out of your mind!" they said.* [Acts 12:15] It seems doubt was on the menu for dinner that night, first Peter and then Mary and her friends. But Rhoda knew what she'd seen. 'It's Peter,' she insisted. They tried to rationalize. *"It must be his angel."* I'm not sure where the thought came from that God would send an angel to represent Peter rather than Peter himself, but that's what they said. Still Rhoda was adamant. And the pounding at the door indicated that someone was indeed there. Finally, a group of them trouped to the door together to see who was making such a racket. And there Peter stood in all his glory – or lack thereof. And their mouths hung open in amazement. Finally, the words came: 'How did you get here? Did they let you go?' It took quite a bit of effort to calm their exuberance and get his story out. 'An angel came, released my chains, told me to dress and follow him. Kept all the guards in a deep sleep and led me out through the gate he opened. When we got to the street, he disappeared. I don't even know his name. But it was Jesus who set me free. I don't know what tomorrow will bring, but tonight through an amazing miracle, I'm free.'

Then he scurried out the door, calling over his shoulder that he had others to tell of his miraculous release. Peter may have been still telling his story as he chowed bread and gulped wine at his friend's house when the dawning sun burst over the hills. But the soldiers were having a completely different experience. Herod Agrippa was furious. How could this guileless fisherman make such a fool of him? How could he manage to elude the battle-hardened soldiers? Did they take a bribe like the soldiers must have done at Jesus' tomb? Well he wasn't going to pay this rabble off like Pilate did. 'Kill them! Kill them all,' he screamed. And every one of those soldiers met their death for apparently shirking their duty. Still Peter remained free – free to fulfill his role as a fisher of men, free to bring other captives out of their chains of sin and death as Jesus promised when he announced his ministry to the surprised listeners at the synagogue in Luke 4:18.

But the time of reckoning was at hand for Herod Agrippa. He was parading about in all his fine clothes and his silks shone in the sun with such splendor that he looked like a messenger of God. When the crowd began to shout their praises to him, even speaking blasphemously that here was God Himself before them, he did not still their voices; he did not silence their foolish acclaim. Like his reprobate Roman friend, Caligula, he liked the praise, liked to be awarded the title of god. But the Almighty was not amused. *"You must not have any other god but me,"* he told Moses and the children of Israel in Exodus 20:3 and this declaration hadn't wavered. Herod Agrippa, even though he was a practicing Jew, had clearly forgotten this admonition, but God had not. *"Instantly, an angel of the Lord struck Herod with a sickness, because he accepted the people's worship instead of giving the glory to God. So he was consumed with worms and died."* [Acts 12:23] Sin consumed his soul, ate away his body and ended his life in great misery and suffering.

What do these miracles teach us about God? No prison doors can hold Him back. No selfish rulers can prevent His people from preaching. And for us? We should never be surprised when what we pray for, actually happens no matter how unlikely or amazing. And the unsaved? Never stand in the place of God's holiness. The results will be catastrophic. As Peter wrote the suffering church in Asia Minor: *"All praise to God the Father of our Lord Jesus Christ. It is by His great mercy that we have been born again, because God raised Jesus Christ from the dead. Now we live with great expectation"* [1 Peter 1:3]. Let us live in great expectation of what God can do.

Chains are Broken

From its concentration on the ministry of the early apostles, the book of Acts moves on to disclose the works of Paul where more miracles abound. In Acts 13 Paul and his encouraging friend Barnabas traveled together to bring the gospel to the region. Through their united ministry we see once again the strength Jesus indicated came by working in pairs [Luke 10:1]. Even King Solomon counselled the importance of such spiritual accord: *"A person standing alone can be attacked and defeated, but two can stand back-to-back and conquer. Three are even better, for a triple-braided cord is not easily broken"* [Ecclesiastes 4:12].

After preaching across the island of Cyprus, Paul and Barnabas met an interesting fellow, who, although he shared their cultural background, expounded a contradictory message. He was a Jewish sorcerer, an oxymoron if ever there was one. Jewish by birth, but not by faith. Even worse, his twisted message was for hire and he tried to convince the island's governor to reject the life-giving words of Barnabas and Paul to ensure his income or influence wasn't curtailed. Paul, however, would have none of his interference and rebuked him boldly: *"You son of the devil, full of every sort of deceit and fraud, and enemy of all that is good! Will you never stop perverting the true ways of the Lord? Watch now, for the Lord has laid his hand of punishment upon you, and you will be struck blind. You will not see the sunlight for some time."* [Acts 13:10-11] By the Holy Spirit's power, the same darkness he was teaching, now covered his eyes, and the governor, upon seeing this miracle believed.

Can you imagine the impact on the region with a governor faithful to Christ for *"wise and knowledgeable leaders bring stability"* we read in Proverbs 28:2. This miracle reminds us to pray for our spiritual and national leaders [1 Thessalonians 5:12,13; Hebrews 13:7,17; 1 Timothy 2:2] for their influence is vast and their testimony can impact policies and people in profound and eternal ways.

We're not told what happened to Elymas, the Jewish sorcerer, but we can only pray that as with Paul's salvation experience with blindness [Acts 9], he came to Christ as a result of the encounter. Nonetheless, like Paul, we need to speak out against deceivers who attempt to pervert the Word of God and hinder its proclamation, for unchecked their spiritual deception can draw people from active faith. In fact, further in this chapter we see the consequence of those who are viciously fighting against the Word of God and its power. In their anger, they even chased Barnabas and Saul from their city, and this would be the experience of these men in city after city – a hungry crowd and a bitter mob.

Yet it seemed that every site of rejection brought an equal or greater assembly of believers. It was while they were in Lystra that scripture records the healing of a man crippled from birth [Acts 14], but this miracle had drastic consequences. The crowd, worshippers of Greek gods, declared Paul and Barnabas were physical representations of these deities, asserting Barnabas was Zeus and Paul was Hermes. Paul was horrified that the work of God would be blasphemously attributed to mythological beings, but his efforts to rectify their misconceptions only incited a riot. Paul was stoned and dragged from the city by Jews believing he was dead. Yet we read: *"as the believers gathered around him, he got up and went back into town"* [Acts 14:20]. God restored his life once again, and we see the fruit of this repeated in Acts 16.

Paul was now travelling with his friend Silas and they'd reached Philippi where they led a wealthy businesswoman, Lydia, to the Lord, and her entire household was baptized. But as we've seen with the Jewish sorcerer Elymas, where God is at work bringing life, the enemy tries to bring death. A slave girl, whose spirit of divination brought great profits to her masters, relentlessly trailed after them shouting: *"These men are servants of the Most High God, and they have come to tell you how to be saved."* [Acts 16:17]

Although her message appeared sound, the messenger was troubled and incurred both disrepute and distraction to Paul's ministry. Her cries became so disruptive that Paul commanded the demon to leave her. Instantly she was free, a fact which meant new life for her, but enraged her owners, for her ability to earn them money vanished with her demon of divination. In their anger, they incited their fellow business men against Paul and Silas, resulting in a vicious beating and imprisonment for them.

Can you imagine the agony they must have been in? Bruises and welts throughout their body. Their inflamed muscles cramped from the stocks clamped over their hands and feet. Most of us would have been moaning in pain. But not Paul and Silas. They were loudly worshipping God so all could hear. They weren't embittered by their circumstances but electrified; they weren't disillusioned but inspired. They turned their prison into a pulpit. And what happened? An earthquake!

A shaking so violent that their stocks burst open, and their prison doors flew off their hinges. The jailor, awakened by the clamor, believed all his prisoners had fled and prepared to fall upon his sword. Paul, sensing this God-given moment, called to the jailor and reassured him that all the inmates were - unbelievably - still there. It was as if a holy hush had fallen upon those in the building. The jailor knew immediately that this was the work of God, for nothing like this could possibly have occurred without God's intervention. His immediate request: *"Sirs, what must I do to be saved?"* [Acts 16: 30]. And at that moment salvation transformed his life and spread to his entire family. What happened when Paul and Silas praised instead of pouted – freedom!

From the worst situation, God brought about the best possible result. From Paul and Silas' imprisonment and torture, God brought about the salvation of the jailer and his family. He even dramatically released the other prisoners for all to see the power of God. Would the city of Philippi ever forget his visit? Not likely. Perhaps that's why Paul's letter to the Philippians contains the repeated advice to rejoice.

What an incredible series of events. Just imagine what can happen when we praise God and preach His Word. Miracles. Let's be part of that.

A Shipwreck Miracle

From his cataclysmic visit to Philippi, Paul traveled across many regions teaching people about Jesus and meeting interest as well as opposition. Diseases were healed and evil spirits were expelled. It was undisputedly the power of God at work through his life. But where light abounds, darkness tries to conceal it. Yet Paul persevered, strengthened by God's directive to testify in Jerusalem and Rome [Acts 23:11].

Even though forty Jews plotted to kill him, God arranged for Paul's nephew to overhear the plans for an ambush and warned the commander. The commander, concerned for the safety of a Roman citizen, organized a heavily armed guard to protect Paul, thereby ensuring that he would face Felix the governor [Acts 23,24]. Like Joseph of the Old Testament, for the next two years Paul remained as Felix's prison guest in order to have repeated opportunities to present the gospel to him. These incidences confirm God's intricate protection and proclamation plans. He is always carefully orchestrating events for us to bring Him glory [Isaiah 43:7]. Let's always be watchful and aware of what He's doing. Sometimes we think we're in prison when in actual fact God has given us a pulpit. Let's make sure we use it.

Determined to see him dead, the Jews brought their accusations to Felix's replacement, Porcius Festus who offered Paul the chance to defend himself in Jerusalem. But Paul knew that death awaited him on that journey, and, assured that God wanted him to testify in

Rome, appealed to Caesar. This request brought about his next series of adventures: shipwreck, serpents and sickness. There is so much to learn in these events. We can begin in Chapter 27. Luke had joined Paul by this time as we see by the first-person account that Luke personally narrated.

The voyage was fraught with trials from the beginning, just as Paul had warned them [Acts 27:10]. Unfortunately, the captain and the ship's owner ignored his prophetic advice, and in favorable weather, they commenced their journey. Yet almost immediately a storm battered their craft. Fortunately, the sailors didn't throw Paul overboard with the cargo as Jonah's shipmates did, and there are no whales in this tale, nor Jonah's disobedience and complaining.

For days the ship was buffeted by a ferocious storm, and nearly starved, the crew believed that all was lost, but Paul knew God wasn't finished with him yet [Acts 27: 21-26], and encouraged them that an angel had assured him that all lives would be saved if they stayed on board. Inspiring courage is a powerful antidote to fear, and one we can all take to heart when facing our storms. When the day dawned, a speck of land was spotted on the horizon. The captain hoped to guide the ship onto the beach but with the wild waves bashing it toward shore, the ship rammed against a sandbar and began to break apart.

The soldiers, as per their instructions, raised their swords to kill all the prisoners, but their commanding officer sought to spar Paul's life and stayed their hand. Two hundred and seventy-six souls leapt into the frothy waters and unbelievably, just as God promised, all of them made it safely to shore. It was a miracle of equal proportions to the 1991 sinking of the cruise ship Oceanos off the coast of South Africa when a raging storm could have resulted in catastrophic loss, yet all 571 people were rescued. Even today, God continues His amazing interventions.

Sopping wet and crusty from salt water as well as exhausted from fighting the crushing waves, Paul made it to shore where yet another test awaited him. As he was gathering firewood, a poisonous snake wiggled out from the fire and sunk its venomous fangs onto Paul's hand, seeping its poison into his system. 'Ha, justice is served' thought those who witnessed the event [Acts 28:3-6], but Paul merely shook it off into the fire and went on with his task. He knew his calling – preach in Rome – and nothing was going to stop him no matter how hard the enemy tried. Not soldiers, not shipwreck, certainly not a serpent. How willing are we to persevere despite difficulties? Do we say we better stop now before things get even worse, or do we turn our faces into the wind, and press on? Paul's life teaches us this lesson. How can we experience miracles if we give up?

It was in fact this miracle that opened the hearts of the Maltese people and made them willing to listen and receive the gospel. Thus, when the father of Publius, the area leader, contracted dysentery, he asked Paul for help. And consider this: God carried Paul through a storm, a shipwreck and a serpent's attack to minister to this elderly man and through him, all the island people, for when they witnessed his healing, they brought all those who were sick to Paul for healing.

What do these miracles show us? The miracle of the elderly man's healing was to relieve suffering, but it was also to show the gentle hand of God. When Paul shook off the viper and remained unaffected from the poison, it was not meant for us to tempt God and try it ourselves to prove our faith or courage. Rather it was to show us how to deal with the enemy. Scripture often refers to Satan as a snake. We see his efforts in the Garden as he curls around the tree and uses his forked tongue to indicate the tempting fruit to Eve. What could she and her husband have done to avoid the fall? James tells us simply to resist the devil and he will flee [James 4:7]. Moreover, Paul tells us that God prepares a way of escape from every temptation: *"The temptations in your life are no different from what others experience. And God is faithful. He will not allow the temptation to be more than you can stand. When you are tempted, he will show you a way out so that you can endure"* [1 Corinthians 10:13].

When the enemy comes against us, we need to take our lesson from these experiences and shake off the enemy, drop him back into the flames as Paul did and get about the business of serving God. Finally, when storms and trials beset us and try to shipwreck us from the ways of God, we need to stand firm, listen carefully to the counsel of the Holy Spirit, and believe that He will give us the strength to master the waves – no matter how high they are. Soon we will find that our feet can touch the bottom, and we can pull ourselves onto dry land.

God doesn't always take us through our Red Seas, but perhaps through the deep waters. Just as God spoke through Isaiah: *"When you go through deep waters, I will be with you. When you go through rivers of difficulty, you will not drown. When you walk through the fire of oppression, you will not be burned up; the flames will not consume you."* [Isaiah 43:2]

Through Paul's life we learn not to give up, but to press on as he wrote in his letters to the Corinthians: *"We are pressed on every side by troubles, but we are not crushed. We are perplexed, but not driven to despair"* [2 Corinthians 4:8], and the Philippians: *"I press on to reach the end of the race and receive the heavenly prize for which God, through Christ Jesus, is calling us"* [Philippians 3:14].

Paul pressed on. Three months later they secured another ship and set sail again and at last Paul reached Rome. After being allotted his own housing, along with his friendly guards, he asked to speak to the prominent Jews of the city. For two years, Paul preached and souls were saved. For two years he endured imprisonment to ensure that captives were set free.

Beloved, today we can be a part of God's redemption plan. All it takes is for us to share the love of God with others, pray for the sick, and press through the waves of persecution. Victory will come and even now is on its way. All we must do is press on.

Wonder of the Word

In looking at the miracles of the New Testament, I was reminded of the miracle that is the Word of God itself. The book we know as the Bible was written by approximately 40 men from a broad range of cultures, educational levels, languages and backgrounds. Its construction spanned 1600 years, from 1500 BC to AD 100.

The Bible contains 66 books, 39 in the Old Testament and 27 in the New Testament. The King James Version that many of us still use or certainly grew up with was commissioned by the King of England and written by dedicated scholars who studied the earlier translations of William Tyndale and others. Published over 400 years ago in 1611, it was based on the Hebrew Bible composed by faithful ancient scribes. The New Testament came to us from Greek texts written by early church writers such as Paul, John, Matthew, Peter and Luke.

These texts have been amazingly saved over countless centuries. Several secular scholars such as Josephus, a Jewish historian, and Tacitus, a Roman historian, have confirmed the events recorded in the New Testament as have other ancient manuscripts provided by writers from the various dynasties who wrote their own monarchy's history and thus supported the events recorded in the Old Testament.

The Bible's unique and infallible words give us literally the Word of God. It contains the phrase "thus saith the Lord" over 3,000 times providing us with God's statement about creation, guidance, judgement, and love. Over 3,200 verses are dedicated to fulfilled prophecy which has occurred during Bible times and over 3,100 verses recount prophecy yet to be fulfilled like we see in much of Revelation.

No book has had so many readers, and reports indicate that it is a continual best seller with the United States alone selling or giving away 168,000 every day. Furthermore, it has been translated into more than 1,200 languages and many have devoted their lives to translating the Bible or portions of it for peoples of various unreached regions. It is generally the first text many of these areas ever receive.

Now that we know what a miraculous book we use as our guide for life, we can look at the miracles recorded in the book of Genesis, the book of beginnings. Shall I remind us of the description of creation: *"In the beginning God created the heavens and the earth. The earth was formless and empty, and darkness covered the deep waters. And the Spirit of God was hovering over the surface of the waters. Then God said, "Let there be light," and there was light. And God saw that the light was good. Then he separated the light from the darkness. God called the light "day" and the darkness "night". And evening passed and morning came, marking the first day"* [Genesis 1:1-5].

From here God proceeds to create the sky and the waters, sun and moon, the land and seas, trees and grasslands, fish and birds, animals and people, and after each miraculous event we read that God declared it was good. God created everything in its precise order and its perfect form so His world could move on its orbit, through its seasons, transitioning from day and night so that all He placed on the earth could flourish. Have you ever taken the time to study the intricacy of a flower or the beauty of a butterfly? Each tiny portion and swirl of color are hand painted by the finger of God. What delight He must have taken when He fashioned each wonder.

There are many web sites and videos that explain creation from a scientific point of view. I tried to search for some useful titbits to share with you, like the specific placement of the earth in the universe so that it would be able to sustain life and be protected from meteorite spray that would have crushed it eons ago, or the protective umbrella of our atmosphere that allows for the production of oxygen so that we can breath and carbon dioxide so that plant life is sustained. Then we have the oceans and the waves cresting the shores, but only in rare instances ever exceeding them or the rainfall which ensures our survival and the regeneration of plants so that every form of animal life can endure.

But God was not finished when He created our globe, when, with His hands He created this perfect sphere with its beautiful swirls of blue and green when seen from space. Yet despite its magnificence, His ultimate creation was humanity. Desiring an intimate, familial relationship He created a living person, to watch over and care for His creation, a perfect match to work in harmony for this purpose.

At each of these moments of creation, from the heavens and the earth through to Adam and Eve, God fashions such amazing, finely tuned, perfectly orchestrated, supremely functioning inter-connective elements that harmonize to reflect not the mischance of fate, or happenstance of cataclysmic events, but the incredible wisdom of a Master Craftsman. Whether we study creation science or the wonder of the human body, we realize that where we live and how we are made, reverberate with the hum of life whispered from the breath of God.

I encourage you this day to stop for a moment and look around you. Look at the sky and its canvas of blue and smudges of white or the perfect curved line of the horizon verifying were earth and sky meet. Gaze at the myriad of greens that sprout from the soil and even look closer at the tiny creatures that flutter, crawl or squiggle about. All have been fashioned by the hand of God. Then gaze into the face of your friend or loved one. Each organ, cell, enzyme has been specifically made by our loving God to create the wonder before you.

How can we doubt that our Redeemer lives when all about us creation shouts His name? Eleven times in Psalm 148 we are told to praise the Lord. What better way to swing into the miracles of the Old Testament than to look at the miracle that is His Word and the wonder of His world. As members of His creation, we can open every day with praise.

Through the Flood

In the same way the Genesis account of the creation has undergone severe scrutiny by scientists who wish to debunk Christ's involvement in the miracles of these events, so, too, the study of Noah's ark and the flood have similarly experienced centuries of scientific and biblical inspection. Over the years I've read many reports by those who've claimed that they've found the Ark's final resting place and remnants of the craft, but the locations keep changing. In case you think that I am trying to soft-sell the flood miracle, I most definitely am not. I believe that God, all powerful, all knowing and ever-present, is capable of the flood and it's nothing but a snap of the fingers for Him. What is amazing is that those with finite human minds could decide that our God, who possesses infinite ability and wisdom, can be limited or debunked by the incomplete and imperfect mind of those beings He created.

But that is not the crux of our discussion today. We're looking at the flood story. What does God say about the miracle of the flood? It begins in Genesis 6 when God is forced to look at the single-minded rebellion of his human creation where *"everything they thought or imagined was consistently and totally evil."* [Genesis 6:5] Feels like our day and age, doesn't it? And like now, God wasn't happy with the mess; in fact: *"It broke his heart."* [Genesis 6:6]. How tragic that our Lord felt that way. After all His effort with the Father and the Holy

Spirit in making this magnificent creation, His children were not only rebellious, but wicked. The sorrow He must have experienced, yet He found one man who sought Him and earned His favor. Noah shunned the evil around him and chose God's companionship instead. Thus, God spoke to Noah about the situation and His solution: A flood is coming! Build a boat!

What makes this so incredible? For one thing, God asked him to build a boat, a very large boat as a matter of fact, then he had to bring pairs of animals into the boat with him, while God flooded the earth. There had never been such a boat constructed before; there had never been such a collection of animals and there had never been a flood. All these things were reason for Noah to question what God was saying, but he didn't. He simply listened and obeyed.

The task took Noah almost 75 years to complete; after all, it was only his family involved in building the ark for no one else believed God. It was a huge undertaking. The Ark, according to the dimensions God stipulated, was three stories high and its area equaled the size of thirty-six tennis courts or twenty college basketball courts. It wasn't until 1884 that people were able to build a more spacious craft when they constructed the Italian liner Eturia.

Thus, it was only Noah, Shem, Ham and Japheth cutting, sawing, and hammering together a vehicle of salvation. Throughout the time, Noah tried to speak to the people around him, but they mocked and condemned him as though he was crazy. 'A flood,' they scoffed, 'God spoke to you?' they sneered. Noah's faithful and persistent message fell on deaf ears. Isaiah commented on such stubborn people [Isaiah 6:9] as did Jesus [Matthew 13:13]. Yet even people's indifference is never a reason for us not to speak for Paul instructs us that how can they call, believe or hear unless someone tells them [Romans 10:14].

After long years of labor, at last everything was ready. Yet the sky was still a brilliant blue, the sun was shining brightly as clouds floated lazily by. Despite the physical evidence of another beautiful day, God told Noah to enter the ark along with his family and the collected pairs of animals. I personally believe that Noah didn't have to run out and find a pair of rabbits hopping by, grab a slithery mom and dad snake or even a couple of eagles or elephants for that matter. I trust that God had already selected the pairs and instructed them to wend their way to Noah just at the right time. Together they all entered the ark and God closed the door behind them. Then seven days later the torrent began and for forty days and nights rain pounded on the roof. Over time, those enclosed in the ark could feel the vessel lifting off the ground and begin to gently sway in the swirling water's swells.

Before it was over, the waters had risen two stories above the highest mountains and for 150 days Noah and his family along with the animals were cocooned safely within the Ark. Jokes have been made about the smell and the tedium of keeping such a craft clean with all its host of animals, and it's humorous to think about, but despite these challenges Noah and his family persevered and were preserved.

In anticipation that the world was dry enough to emerge, Noah sent out a raven, but it never returned. Noah then released a dove which returned with an olive branch clutched in its tiny beak, this tiny twig an indication that the earth was sprouting again. Thus, today it is the dove and not the raven that is the global symbol for peace, for God used this gentle, selfless creature to bring the message that a peaceful resting place was available.

At last it was time to leave. The world was washed clean and Noah and his family were ready to start their lives anew. In heartfelt thanksgiving Noah built an altar and offered a sacrifice to God for His miraculous redemption. It's with this sacrifice that God promised Noah - and us: *"I am confirming my covenant with you. Never again will floodwaters kill all living creatures; never again will a flood destroy the earth."* [Genesis 9:11]

What does this mean for us? No matter how long it rains or how high the waters climb, God assures us that the entire earth will not be flooded. As a guarantee, God places a rainbow in the sky, painting brilliant ribbons of light to ark across the horizon, declaring to all who see it that although it might rain, the sun will reappear.

From this story, we don't need to be caught up in the debate of what is or isn't. We can simply have faith in what God says and believe Him. When He says, 'Do the impossible. Build an ark.' – we can do it no matter how long it takes or how many criticize our labors. When He shows us a way of escape – we must take it. Even if the sun seems to be shining, He knows that there are storms 'acomin'. Then when He sets our feet on dry ground, we can rejoice at His deliverance and celebrate with sacrifices of praise for even then more promises await.

The Miracle of Speech

Have you ever considered the power of language? Words can make us feel good about ourselves or deflate us like a balloon. They have the power to marry us, send us to jail or award us a university degree. Words help us get and keep our jobs, begin and end friendships, get sick or stay healthy as it says in Proverbs 16:24: *"Kind words are like honey— sweet to the soul and healthy for the body."* They can speak a blessing or deliver a curse as James warns in 3:10.

Wow! Words are powerful tools. God understood their potential. When the earth was formless and void, God spoke the words: *"Let there be light"* [Genesis 1:3] and darkness evaporated and light blinked into existence. When God searched His creation and found that there was no living creature with whom He could have a close and meaningful relationship, He spoke the words: *"Let us make human beings in our image, to be like Us"* [Genesis 1:26] and then God created people, the very heart of His heart. He developed prayer for the very purpose of being able to communicate with Him.

Sometimes though, our words are not gardens of delight but cesspools of decay. Proverbs 12:6 explains their influence: *"The words of the wicked are like a murderous ambush, but the words of the godly save lives."* Later Solomon added: *"The tongue can bring death or life; those who love to talk will reap the consequences"* [Proverbs 18:21]. Perhaps He was thinking about this when he administered his judgement

concerning the two mothers who were arguing over one living baby
[1 Kings 3:27]. Through his words, he guaranteed life for the infant
and his mother.

But our words don't just determine our current situations, they
determine our destiny and our eternity. Jesus explains: *"And I tell you
this, you must give an account on judgment day for every idle word you
speak. The words you say will either acquit you or condemn you"* [Matthew
12:36-37]. Therefore, we need to consider carefully how and what we
speak. The health of our relationships depends upon them: *"A gentle
answer deflects anger, but harsh words make tempers flare... Gentle words
are a tree of life; a deceitful tongue crushes the spirit"* [Proverbs 15:1,4].

Jesus, whose words were always gracious [Luke 4:22] cautions that
our mouth reveals our hearts and used the Pharisees as His example
[Matthew 12:34]. Furthering this counsel, the Apostle Paul provides
specific instruction about words in his letters to the churches. To the
Romans he warns that the ungodly have foul mouths which spew
venom like a snake [Romans 3:13]. To the Colossians [3:16] he advises
thankful worship and recommends that their conversation is gracious
and attractive [Colossians 4:6]. To the Ephesians he is more direct,
warning them to *"stop telling lies"* [4:25] and choose inspiring words
instead [Ephesians 4:29].

A sweet little poster I've seen shows a little gerbil chewing away on
a piece of lettuce. The caption says: 'Be careful of the words you say, for
you may have to eat them'. I've often thought of that phrase as a sign
that my words may come back to haunt me, so I best show restraint
before I have to ask forgiveness. I wish I could say I always do, but I
am sincerely trying.

Well, you may ask, how does this discussion of words relate to
miracles in the Old Testament. I'm sure we all recall the story of the
Tower of Babel described in Genesis 11. Here was a time when *"everyone
in the world spoke the same language and used the same words"* [verse 1].
But it wasn't for the purpose of building one another up or for praising
God. It was to illustrate their power and to place themselves on par with
God. They wanted to be famous. They wanted everyone to see how
great, clever and industrious they were. Their actions had nothing to do

with God and God knew it; He saw their prideful heart. He knew that their desires revealed their willfulness and more so He knew that their efforts would yield destruction. Thus, He muddled their language, forcing them to find like-minded speakers and together wander off to settle their own regions.

Do you recall God's original instructions? They were to take care of the whole earth, not the tiny area where they were still huddled together. God wants us united, yes, but under His banner of love and peace, not our personal banner of selfishness and pride. He shows us how this is to be done in Acts 2 when, through the power of His Holy Spirit, He unites all people through the message of redemption. He overcame at Pentecost the difficulty of language by giving the disciples the gift of speaking other languages. How interesting if you notice that when we read of the Holy Spirit touching each of those in the Upper Room it is with *tongues* of fire. God gave them tongues of fire and then set their tongues alight with the fire of His Word so His message could be delivered in languages that the visitors to the area could understand.

What then are we to do with our words? We are to use them to glorify God, build relationships, encourage others and resolve conflicts. We are also to use them to share the gospel [Deuteronomy 11:18; Romans 10:9,10; Romans 15:6; 1 Peter 3:15]. Let us begin today by practicing our testimony [Revelations 12: 11] and learning the word of God so we can speak its life to everyone who will hear.

The Miracle of God's Selection

The miracle of God's selection. We witness it when God notices Noah [Genesis 6:8]. Despite everyone around him being wicked, and their entire focus on evil, Noah turned his face to God; he chose the moments of his day to "*walk in close fellowship with God.*" [Genesis 6:9] This is even more remarkable because he had no one around him teaching him the Bible. No one except his family with whom to fellowship. No other resource to sustain his faith, except his own determined commitment to remain close with God.

In a time when we have ready access to any number of Bible translations and inspirational texts, services any day of the week, internet and television programs to encourage our faith, Noah's unwavering commitment to God is remarkable. It is no wonder that God selected him for such an amazing task, literally to save the world and reestablish it under the Lord's direction.

The miracle of God's selection happens again and again in scripture. Genesis 12 directs us to yet another of God's choices. In the godless nation of Ur of the Chaldees, God saw a man who unlike everyone in his area, looked to God for provision and direction. Thus, God called him, instructing him to leave his homeland and travel to an unknown destination of His choosing. God selected Abraham to be blest and to be a blessing.

Why him? Abraham's home city, Ur, was a wealthy, prosperous

city of approximately 24,000 people who worshipped many gods, but especially the moon god Nanna. The region was highly advanced boasting markets, schools, libraries, lush gardens and even universities. These Chaldeans were very spiritual people who offered sacrifices to Nanna in the many temples they constructed for worship. It was from this highly civilized, culturally and spiritually expressive city that Abraham was called by God.

As a prosperous businessman, Abraham had to leave behind his home, friends and economic security to head out into an unknown, dangerous territory with only the certainty of God's calling. Remarkably, even Sarah his wife was willing to go without question or resistance. Unlike Lot's wife, she did not look back, but moved with her husband, willing to live in tents, travel as nomads with no fixed location, surrounded by hostile forces. Yet God selected Abraham to be a blessing and to bring a blessing to untold generations of similar people of faith who were willing to follow God sight unseen.

Throughout their journey, God saw Abraham's faith and continued to speak to him. He repeated His covenant promise in Genesis 15 and 17: 4 *"This is my covenant with you: I will make you the father of a multitude of nations!"* Thus, in Abraham's life we see the miracle of God's selection, a choosing that involves not only a close relationship with God, but a destiny of service and ministry that blesses countless generations as well.

Moses is another that was selected as we read in Psalm 106:23: *"Moses, his chosen one, stepped between the Lord and the people. He begged him to turn from his anger and not destroy them."* Moses was chosen to lead the children of Israel out of bondage, guide them through the Red Sea, direct them to the Promised Land, and intercede for them when their disobedience almost cost them their lives.

Similarly, those of the tribe of Levi were chosen to serve God in the sanctuary: *"I myself have chosen your fellow Levites from among the Israelites to be your special assistants. They are a gift to you, dedicated to the Lord for service in the Tabernacle."* [Numbers 18:6]. Deuteronomy 14:2 stresses their holy selection: *"You have been set apart as holy to the Lord your God, and he has chosen you from all the nations of the earth to be his own special treasure".* The book of Chronicles indicates the Levites were to carry the Ark, lead worship, guard the Ark, blow the trumpets, as well as play the worship instruments. With their divinely endowed responsibilities came a warning: *"My sons, do not neglect your duties any longer! The Lord has chosen you to stand in his presence, to minister to him, and to lead the people in worship and present offerings to him."* [2 Chronicles 29:11] The directives given to the Levites are similar to those given to contemporary worship leaders, pastors and lay ministry leaders.

Other men chosen by God in the Old Testament include David [1 Kings 8:16] and Solomon [1 Chronicles 28:10]. Yet God's choosing extends beyond individuals to entire tribes as we read in Isaiah 43:10: *"But you are my witnesses, O Israel!" says the Lord. "You are my servant. You have been chosen to know me, believe in me, and understand that I alone am God. There is no other God— there never has been, and there never will be."*

What about our calling, our selection, God's choosing of us? Matthew 22:14 says that *"many are called, but few are chosen".* In pondering this verse, it seems almost contradictory to the previous verses we've looked at. But let's think more deeply. At my university, a 'call' is often given for students to apply for a particular bursary and students are welcome to put their name and qualifications forth to request it. Similarly, a company may place an ad which calls people to apply for a particular position.

Similarly, God gives a call to people to come to Him; then He gives a call for people to serve Him in specific ways. After His spectacular vision of the Lord, Isaiah hears a call: *"Then I heard the Lord asking, "Whom should I send as a messenger to this people? Who will go for us?" I said, "Here I am. Send me"* [Isaiah 6:8]. When he answered the call of God, Isaiah was chosen to be His messenger. It works the same with us.

Have you sensed a call from God to serve Him in a particular way; have you felt a longing to worship him, serve in hospitality, tell others about him, encourage others in their faith, provide for the needs of others. God has undoubtedly chosen you for these rewarding areas of ministry, and you will only be fulfilled when you actively respond to the call God has given you.

2 Chronicles 16:9 tells us that "*The eyes of the LORD search the whole earth in order to strengthen those whose hearts are fully committed to him.*" This verse first came to my attention during the Keith Green Memorial concerts. Keith Green, a gifted singer and songwriter, dedicated father and husband, and a dynamic Christian leader felt compelled to inspire young people into missionary service. Sadly, he was tragically killed in a plane crash along with two of his young children, his pilot and another young family of six. His wife, who was carrying their fourth child, had remained at home with their toddler and thus was saved from this tragedy. Undoubtedly her grief was overwhelming, but she shared her husband's passion for the lost and his desire to see young people mobilized for missions. Thus, she continued the concert tours her husband had organized and at the end of each night sang this verse to inspire those in the audience to answer God's call.

Their lives, their choices illustrate the miracle of God's selection. Our heavenly Father surveys His world seeking those who seek Him. Searching for those who desire to serve Him with their whole heart using the gifts, resources and energies He's given them.

Has this stirred something in you today? Does the miracle of God's selection inspire you to answer His call? When you hear Him ask: 'will you do this for me', will you answer: 'Here I am'? God searches the world over for people who are willing. Is that you? Will you answer His call?

The Miracle of God's Protection

Have you ever thought: 'How did God find me' or 'How did I find God?' Perhaps you are from a family where there is no one else who has a strong relationship with Christ. This absence of spiritual commitment or even interest makes you wonder how your heart turned toward Him. My own family, for the most part, had a quiet church relationship with God, and although they faithfully took me to Sunday School and church, it was through friends that I found the love of Christ promised in His Word. Now, of course, I recognize and thank God for those in my family who prayed for me, despite my rebellious heart.

Lot was that kind of blessed man. He listened to what Abraham said about God's counsel and promises. He watched as Abraham was protected and blessed, but it reached a point when the wealth of Abraham and Lot became so extensive that the area couldn't support all their workers and flocks. Fights broke out between the two groups, and the discord concerned Abraham. To bring peace, Abraham offered Lot the choice of the land that spread out before them. Although Abraham was the elder and the chief of the family, in his graciousness he gave Lot first choice.

Lot's eyes fell to the well-watered and fertile valleys of the Jordan. It was described to be as beautiful and bountiful as the garden of God. Without a moment's thought, Lot stretched out his hand and selected this lush area, leaving Abraham with the dry region of Canaan. But

God saw Abraham's generous heart and rewarded him once again: *"After Lot had gone, the* LORD *said to Abram, "Look as far as you can see in every direction—north and south, east and west. I am giving all this land, as far as you can see, to you and your descendants as a permanent possession. And I will give you so many descendants that, like the dust of the earth, they cannot be counted! Go and walk through the land in every direction, for I am giving it to you".* [Genesis 13:14-16]. It is a promise He fulfilled when Joshua led the children of Israel into the Promised Land.

But what about Lot. His choice, though apparently sensible in the eyes of the world, brought death to his soul for he settled near Sodom, an area inhabited by people who were profoundly wicked. Lot may have selected an area that offered prosperity, but it would starve his soul as he soon came to realize. Robbers came to Sodom and Gomorrah and plundered the cities and people, carrying off everything and everyone, including Lot and his family.

It doesn't pay to be greedy, does it as Proverbs 1:19 and Proverbs 28:20,22 warn us? Fortunately, Lot had a loving uncle who came to his rescue. As soon as Abraham learned that Lot had been kidnapped, he gathered over three hundred trained soldiers, and chased after the marauders, found them, defeated them, freed the captives and reclaimed their stolen possessions.

Did Lot learn from this experience and avoid Sodom and all its wickedness? Did he instead stick close to his God-fearing uncle Abraham? I'm afraid not. He sidled back to Sodom and set up house there with his wife and daughters once again. He even engaged his daughters to men from this city. Yet despite his choices, God was still watching over him, through his uncle Abraham.

When God came to Abraham to deliver the fantastic news that elderly Sarah would have his son, God gave him another important piece of information. He determined not to hide His plans from His friend [Genesis 18: 17-20]. God's selection of Abraham ensured a cherished relationship in which God desired to share meaningful knowledge with him and trusted him to know what to do with it. Naturally, the news of Sodom and Gomorrah's destruction worried Abraham. This was his nephew Lot's home. Surely, he could intervene and ask for mercy, he thought, and thus asked God to stay His hand of judgement if 50, 45, 40, 30, 20, and finally if only 10 righteous people lived in the city.

Have you ever wondered why God gives us insight into a person's life or a situation? This is precisely why God shares news like this with us. It isn't to give us fear, but faith. He wants us to pray and intercede for them, just as Abraham did for Sodom and Gomorrah. Abraham thought surely there were ten people who believed in and loved God in that city. Surely Lot had reached out and touched his neighbors and told them about his faith.

Sadly, though, that wasn't the case. When the angels arrived in the city, only Lot welcomed them. The remaining men demanded the visitors for their sexual pleasure, an action which appalled Lot. He attempted to resist their attack and without the angels' rescue would have succumbed to his neighbors' assault. The revelation of the angelic messengers' divine assignment: the rescue of Lot and the destruction of the city shocked Lot and his family. When Lot tried to warn his daughters' fiancés, they mocked his fervency, and he was forced to bundle only his wife and daughters together to leave the city. Yet he saw his family's reluctance and begged the angelic messengers for more time to escape, which, due to God's merciful nature, he was provided.

When God chooses us, when He places us under the umbrella of His protection, it's amazing what can happen. God was watching over Lot and his family, despite their foolish choices. But His mercy reached to a point. 'Don't look back! Keep running and don't look back.' Yet Lot's wife was torn. She was leaving behind everyone and everything she knew. She couldn't see the freedom and safety before her, only the wealth and security behind and so, despite the sound of thunder, the feel of the heat, the rumble of the ground under her feet guaranteeing that the destruction the angels warned of was actually happening, she stopped and turned. One last longing look, but that was all it took. The breath of life God had placed within her wisped away on a sigh; the water of life coursing through her veins evaporated, and she became a pillar of salt. What a horrible, needless end. Lot's wife became an example of those who refused to look ahead to the freedom God sets before them and longed instead for the death and destruction behind.

Beloved, let us learn from Lot's family. Let us be grateful for family members who pray for us, are generous with us, help us even when we don't deserve it. Let us be careful where we settle and who we surround ourselves with. Their trappings of success may really be only rusted heaps of emptiness. When God makes a way of escape, we need to run to it, and flee into the protective arms of God. We will always be safe there. We mustn't long for the past. It's over and dead to us. We're alive in Christ and need to always look ahead to the freedom He's saved us for.

Overcoming Rejection

Rejection is a terrible thing. It bites into our heart and empties our soul. Sometimes the world can be a very cruel place and the people in it can do things to us that has the potential of changing us forever. But God still has amazing ways to intervene and introduce us to other possibilities of a sweet and tender love that is more special and wonderful than anything the earth can imagine or arrange. Hagar discovered the love of God at a moment in her life when all seemed lost.

We're introduced to this beleaguered young woman in Genesis 16 where we're told that she was an Egyptian maidservant to Sarai, Abraham's beloved but barren wife. In actual fact, Hagar was a slave, forcibly taken into Abraham's household. Slaves were either captives of war or payment for a family debt. What a horrible aftereffect for a young girl to lose her family, her home, her culture and language and become the property of strangers. Abraham's great grandson Joseph would suffer the same fate although he was able to successfully overcome the corrupt plans of Potiphar's wife. Hagar, however, couldn't overcome Sarai's plans for her. This is where we find her.

Sarai was in anguish at not having a child to hold to her breast, dangle on her knee, kiss till the giggles came. But what was even worse was the fact that she'd not been able to give Abraham the son he so wanted. For over ten years God had been speaking to Abraham that he would have children, but her womb had never carried his child. She was frustrated with Abraham's faith, his continuous revelation of God's pronouncements of land, descendants and blessings, and even though Abraham was getting richer by the day, still there was no child.

Well, thought Sarai, if God said that her husband would have a son, then he would have a son. There had to be a solution available, and looking at her beautiful slave, she thought she'd found it. Hagar was a dutiful slave, quiet, hard-working and lovely to look at. Surely, she could produce a child for Sarai with her husband Abraham. This was a common practice in her culture, arranging a surrogate mother to bear a child. Thus, Sarai put her plan in motion. First telling Abraham: *"The LORD has prevented me from having children. Go and sleep with my servant. Perhaps I can have children through her"*, then instructing Hagar to give herself to Abraham [Genesis 16: 2].

Unfortunately, the plan worked too well. Hagar almost immediately became pregnant. Undoubtedly Abraham was overjoyed that he would at last have a child. Perhaps he began to show Hagar greater favor and attention. Whatever happened, Hagar acted scornfully with Sarai which enraged Sarai. Not only had she faced the painful years of barrenness and the pitying looks of other women who could bear numerous children for their husbands, but here now was the further evidence that she was the one who was physically faulty, the one undoubtedly cursed by God with barrenness. In fury she turned on her husband: *"This is all your fault! I put my servant into your arms, but now that she's pregnant she treats me with contempt. The LORD will show who's wrong—you or me!"* [Genesis 16: 5] Abraham was aghast. Without question, he chose his barren wife over her pregnant slave, for he loved his wife and understood her anguish. He made it clear that she would always be first choice in his heart by telling her to do whatever she wished with Hagar. His support was just what Sarai needed to appease her aching heart and thus, she turned on Hagar, treating her so badly that she fled into the desert.

Remember what I said about rejection. Hagar had already felt its sting when she was sold into slavery. Then at last she was able to feel somewhat restored and regain a sense of worth when she was able to carry Abraham's child. Yet pride slipped in, smothered her relationship with Sarai and brought down her fierce anger. Even Abraham, the father of the child she was carrying did not protect her, driving the razor-sharp pain of rejection further into her heart.

Driven by heat and thirst, she found a spring in the wilderness. Yet what a lonely place it was. No food, no home, no friends, no shelter, no support. How she would ever survive? Her hand caressed the small mound of her stomach where the son of Abraham lay cradled. How would her child ever survive? In such a lonely place, with rejection like a vulture sitting heavy on her shoulder, the angel of God found her. *"Hagar, Sarai's servant, where have you come from, and where are you going?"* [Genesis 16:8]. How like God to ask these probing questions which require us to face our fears and our failures. God didn't need to ask her why she was running. He didn't need to be told of Sarai's hateful treatment. He knew everything that had happened and knew what needed to take place next: *"Return to your mistress, and submit to her authority."* [Genesis 16:9]

What a difficult command to hear when you're emotionally and physically vulnerable. But this place of humbling would not be without reward: *"I will give you more descendants than you can count."* Then He explains further: *"You are now pregnant and will give birth to a son. You are to name him Ishmael (which means 'God hears'), for the LORD has heard your cry of distress."* [Genesis 16:11].

Hagar may have only known rejection, but God was showing her selection and protection. 'You will be a special mother with many grandchildren and great grandchildren. Not only that, the baby you now carry is a boy, and his name is to be "God hears" so you may remember that I have heard your lonely cry this day. What's more, this son of yours will be a strong, independent young man who may also face hardships and rejection, but nonetheless he will live for I know his future just as I know yours.'

What a comforting word for Hagar. It changed her entire view of her situation and her understanding of God. As an Egyptian, she'd worshipped foreign gods and very likely hadn't completely embraced the God of Abraham. But knowing God heard her cry for help, she knew He saw her and her needs. She was no longer the rejected one, the ignored one, but one special in the eyes of God, loved by Him.

What happens next? Did everything go smoothly and sweetly after this. Unfortunately not. Hagar did return, bore Abraham a son whom he named Ishmael. Abraham loved this boy, but he was not the one chosen by God as the righteous heir. God visited Abraham once again and told him that even in Sarai's old age she would bear him a son and laughter would be his name for he was their son of promise.

All was well for some time for Abraham loved both of his sons, but time came to celebrate Isaac's weaning from his mother. It's likely that the older boy Ishmael was jealous of his baby brother, certainly he was envious of the great party being thrown in Isaac's honor and scorned the younger child. Sarah was outraged. Maybe she was remembering when Hagar mocked her; perhaps she was looking for an excuse to rid herself of her son's hereditary rival. She turned on her husband again commanding him to cast out Hagar and her contemptuous offspring.

Abraham was heartbroken. He wanted to raise both of his sons, even though he knew that Isaac would be his heir, he wanted to provide for Ishmael as well. In his distress, he went to God for guidance and God made his direction clear: *"Do not be upset over the boy and your servant. Do whatever Sarah tells you, for Isaac is the son through whom your descendants will be counted. But I will also make a nation of the descendants of Hagar's son because he is your son, too."* [Genesis 21:12, 13] Even in this complex family situation, God was working. With a heavy but obedient heart, Abraham sent Hagar and his son back out to the wilderness.

Hagar found herself facing the wilderness again rejected, abandoned, hated. Yet now in this desolate place she had her young son to care for. It was too much. Yet the God who sees was still with her, the God who loves her was still watching over her [Genesis 21: 17,18] In this traumatic moment, God reminded Hagar of His promise of a wonderful future for her son, and He also provided for their present needs, presenting her with a well of rich, refreshing water to sustain them on their journey.

Through the experiences of Hagar, we see that the world may reject us, cast us aside, and leave us abandoned in the wilderness, but even in those dark and lonely places, God finds us, comforts us, calls us, and rescues us. If you have felt the world's rejection, if you have felt that no one cares about you, whether you live or die, know that God has heard your every whimper. He has collected your every tear. He has carved your name on the palm of His hand. He has loved you perfectly and will love you forever. You are never alone. Look and listen and hear His whisper. "Don't be afraid, I am here."

A Miracle Wife

Our story meets up with Abraham's family when he was almost 140 years old; his beloved wife Sarah had already passed away. Now it was time for Isaac to have a wife, but there was no suitable bride available amongst the godless people of Canaan. Abraham called his servant Eliezer, a man who for years had faithfully served him and who, at one time, he'd considered making his heir. However, God had fulfilled His promise of a son and now that son needed a wife. Yet this wife had to be someone who shared their faith and didn't worship the hideous gods around them. Thus, Abraham instructed Eliezer: *"Swear by the LORD, the God of heaven and earth, that you will not allow my son to marry one of these local Canaanite women. Go instead to my homeland, to my relatives, and find a wife there for my son Isaac"* [Genesis 24: 3, 4].

Eliezer realized that he was tasked with a very long and dangerous journey; he knew that it would be extremely difficult to find a suitable bride amongst Abraham's family. They might even demand that Isaac come to them so they could check him out, to determine if he was worthy of their daughter. Yet Abraham was adamant. Under no circumstances was Eliezer to take Isaac back there, for God's promise resided in the land he'd claimed.

In obedience Eliezer undertook the journey of almost 500 miles over sand dunes and through dusty wilderness plains. When he finally arrived at Abraham's brother Nahor's town, the first thing he did once he dismounted from his camel was kneel and pray, asking God to bless his search by providing a woman who would offer to draw water for his thirsty camels. Eliezer strategically dismounted by the village wells, knowing his animals needed to be watered, but also assured that this would be the meeting place where young herders would gather to water their flocks. No sooner had he finished praying than he noticed the women of the area arriving with their herds. It was the end of a very long day in the fields and it was time for their thirsty animals to drink before hustling them into their pens. Undoubtedly these women wanted nothing more than to finish up their chores and head off to their homes for a greatly deserved meal and rest.

Eliezer's prayer seemed like an impossible request. What young woman would make such an offer? He knew that a thirsty camel could consume as much as 30 gallons (135 litres) of water in about 13 minutes which would mean she would have to draw as much as 400 gallons of water to satisfy Eliezer's entourage. Clearly Eliezer was looking for a very special person. Someone who was gracious, hospitable, hardworking and welcoming to strangers. This would be no ordinary woman, but one willing to sacrifice her time and energy without any thought of reward. Just the perfect wife for quiet Isaac. Would Eliezer find such a woman there?

Then Eliezer spotted a beautiful, maidenly woman who graciously responded to Eliezer's request for a drink. Eliezer must have watched this young woman over the rim of the jug, studied her carefully and waited breathlessly to see what she would do next. As he handed back the jug, he heard the words he'd prayed for: *"I'll draw water for your camels, too, until they have had enough to drink."* [Genesis 24: 19] Was this woman the one that God had selected? She was all that Eliezer had prayed for: hard-working, generous, hospitable, welcoming. Moreover, she was beautiful and he could see that she was still unmarried by her attire. As he watched her in silence, Eliezer wondered if God had led him to just the right place and the right person. After rewarding her generosity with jewelry, Eliezer finally asked the important question about her family. Upon learning that she belonged to Abraham's brother's home, Eliezer knew his quest was successful and dropped to his knees in worship.

Rebekah didn't know what to think. After all she was only doing what was in her heart. Without thinking, she ran home to tell her family what had happened. Immediately, her brother, Laban, rushed out to welcome the stranger to their home. Before, Laban could set a meal before him, Eliezer insisted that he explain his mission and reviewed for them the entire story of Abraham's instruction, including his prayerful arrival and Rebekah's faithful and generous response.

Both her brother and father, Bethuel, acknowledged God's hand in this miraculous process and agreed to surrender Rebekah into Eliezer's care. The next morning Eliezer was anxious to return to his master, but Laban and Bethuel tried to detain him. Perhaps they thought the longer he stayed the more he would give them. Knowing what we learn of them later in their treatment of Jacob, it's certainly possible that greed was their motive. Regardless of their reasoning, they called Rebekah before them and asked her to decide if she was ready to go. Without hesitation, Rebekah agreed. She could not help but see that God had selected her for a momentous task. Likely she didn't know who Isaac was; didn't know what her new life would be like, but she was ready for the adventure. She was ready to be a servant in the hand of God to do as He asked.

How do I know this? When they arrived after their long journey, Rebekah saw a young man on the hillside. Isaac walked the fields in prayer every evening as was his custom, no doubt also praying for Eliezer's successful return. When he saw them coming, his heart must have leapt into his throat. Rebekah had the same response. Upon hearing that this was her betrothed, she slid off her camel and respectfully covered her face with a veil. When Eliezer encountered Isaac, he told him the amazing story of God's protection and selection. Protection for He carried them safely across hundreds of miles and selection because He directed Eliezer to the exact woman He'd chosen for Isaac.

Isaac was overwhelmed with joy. We're told that he brought his new bride into his mother's tent and immediately took her to wife.

Moreover, "*he loved her deeply, and she was a special comfort to him after the death of his mother*" [Genesis 24:67]. Since Adam, this is one of the first times that we read of a husband's love for his wife. Abraham was certainly devoted to his wife Sarah and undoubtedly loved her, but we don't read it so directly as we do in the case of Isaac and Rebekah.

God is amazing in His selection and protection. We can look to Him, trust in Him, have faith in Him that what He plans, He can accomplish. A favorite Bible verse explains this: "*For I know the plans I have for you," says the* LORD. "*They are plans for good and not for disaster, to give you a future and a hope.*" [Jeremiah 29:11] Most of us love that verse because it assures us that God is orchestrating events on our behalf that will bless us. When we couple this verse with Romans 8:28: "*God causes everything to work together for the good of those who love God and are called according to His purpose for them*", we realize that He's able to organize amazing miracles to ensure that all that He desires for us will come to pass.

You may be at a place right now where you're uncertain of God's selection and protection. You may wonder if His plans for you are actually for good or if He can work good out of the current situation that you're in. Fear not! He always says. He is on your side, working out even your sorrow for good. Every day you can count on Him even when everything looks bleak. With His presence in your life, all things will truly turn out for good and the miracles He can make happen will bring laughter again to your soul.

The Miracle of Restoration

Brothers and sisters. Sometimes we love them – sometimes we don't. The Word gives us advice on turning problematic relationships into peaceful friendships. Seems impossible sometimes, doesn't it, but as we study the miracle that God did in Esau and Jacob's lives it should give us hope of what He can do in our potentially broken bonds.

Literally from the womb Jacob and Esau were fighting with one another. Rebekah was so concerned for the wrestling going on inside her womb, she pleaded with God for answers. God explained to her the nations that were struggling to emerge from within her [Genesis 25:22, 23]. God knew what was happening and what would happen. Did He create enmity between them? No, He didn't. Despite their physical closeness, even in the womb, they found reasons to disagree. Even there they couldn't appreciate one another's differences but found them offensive. I hope this doesn't sound familiar - but it might.

As they were born, the wrestling continued as to who would be first, with the younger grasping the firstborn's heel. Even their parents found their unique qualities reason to choose one over the other. Rebekah liked Jacob's quiet, obedient, respective demeanor that kept him closer to home. Isaac preferred Esau, his rough and tumble oldest son because he liked the outdoors and appreciated Esau's independent, boisterous spirit. Did you notice that these parents actually preferred the child that exhibited the very qualities they didn't possess? Isaac, you recall was a quiet, peace-loving man whereas Rebekah was an adventurous woman willing to travel countless miles to meet and marry her husband.

Anyone who has read about parenting or been parented knows the heartache of having a mom or dad who favored one sibling over another. Only the unconditional love of Jesus can heal that kind of hurt. Unfortunately, Isaac and Rebekah hadn't read any parenting manuals or learned from their own life experiences. Remember that Isaac was the chosen son whereas Ishmael his brother was the son abandoned to the wilderness. Unfortunately, Isaac didn't consider the pain inflicted on Ishmael or perhaps he wouldn't have favored the one who made the tastiest meals of wild game and leave his youngest to the counsel of his wife.

The rivalry foretold by God while the sons were in the womb, appeared full blown when they became young men. It was possible, even likely, that Rebekah had told Jacob what God had promised: the oldest would serve the younger, for at the first opportunity Jacob demanded the rights of a firstborn. Do you remember the story? Esau arrived home from a day of hunting, exhausted and hungry and demanded his sibling fetch him stew. Perhaps it was in jest, or perhaps it was in the hopes of obtaining the promise, whatever the case, Jacob demanded Esau pay for his meal with his firstborn birthright.

What's the big deal you may ask? We don't really use this term today or recognize its significance, but for Jacob and Esau there was an important and sizeable benefit for being the oldest son. In biblical times the firstborn son was allocated a double portion of the inheritance and assigned the role of head of the family, assuming his father's position, including his rights and responsibilities upon his death. Obviously, this was something that Jacob desperately wanted and believed that he spiritually deserved. Conversely Esau could care less, moaning that since he was perishing from starvation, why not pay this miniscule price. But Jacob wasn't satisfied with Esau's flippant, frustrated response requiring him to swear to give him the birthright. Esau didn't blink an eye but immediately gave away his sacred birthright.

Sometime later the relationship between the brothers took another downward turn. Isaac was aging and his eyesight was gone.

Unconcerned that Esau had despised his birthright, Isaac decided that he could still pronounce a blessing over his firstborn. He sent Esau out to hunt for meat and commanded him to prepare a favorite stew. Rebekah saw this as her opportunity. Having overheard Isaac's instruction, she commanded Jacob to prepare and present a tasty stew for his father. Jacob worried that even blind his father would be able to tell his sons apart and pronounce a curse on Jacob for his deception, but Rebekah was adamant, offering even to take the curse upon herself to ensure that her beloved son would receive the blessing.

Lies and deception. That was definitely not what God intended when He spoke the word to Rebekah decades before. This is a warning to us all that we must be careful to avoid forcing God's word into our reality and instead let His power accomplish His Will. Yet Jacob, through the timely delivery of a delicious stew, and the false attire and hairy arms to mimic his brother, received the coveted blessing comprising abundant wealth, power and protection, all the things that Esau was expecting to receive.

Esau howled in anguish when he heard what Jacob had stolen from him, especially in light of what he was promised: isolation and servitude, until finally he'd break free. Esau raged, vowing to kill his brother after Isaac died. In fear, Jacob fled from his family and for the next twenty years endured the deception and cruelty of his obnoxious Uncle Laban. Ironically, Jacob suffered under the guiles of an uncle who more than repaid him for his own earlier deceptions. Moreover, for two decades he received nothing from the inheritance and blessing of the first born that he'd fought so hard to achieve.

When at last Jacob decided to flee the tyranny of his uncle and return home to Canaan and whatever family was left to him, Jacob had no idea what his brother Esau would do to him. When he heard that Esau was heading his way with 400 soldiers, he believed that Esau would finally fulfill his threats from years ago. Hoping to appease his brother, he prepared a generous gift of goats, sheep, cattle, camels and donkeys. Yet time and experience had also taught him to seek God's mercy and protection as well.

Fortunately, God had already worked in Esau's heart. Revenge was no longer his quest for he'd seen God's blessing and protection in his own life. The influence and love of his father had changed him into a man seeking peace not payback. Like the story of the prodigal son, before Jacob even reached Esau, Esau ran forward and embraced his estranged brother [Genesis 33:4]. It was a poignant and memorable reunion which brought both men to tears. Not only did Esau not retaliate, but he also declined the gifts, assuring Jacob that he'd already acquired a massive fortune of his own. Then when Esau offered Jacob and his entourage a military escort, Jacob graciously declined stating that Esau's welcome was reward enough. This amazing exchange illustrates the depth and breadth of complete reconciliation. Not only had Esau forgiven him, but he wanted to ensure Jacob's safety and desired that they live together in peace and harmony not in rivalry and jealousy.

From the lives of Jacob and Esau we see the wonder of God performing a miracle in hearts and lives that only He can do to ensure that anger and hatred aren't carried to the grave. Through their restored relationship, we see the miracles that God can do in all broken relationships. No matter how tattered and torn they've become or what one person has done or said to the other, God is able to restore, renew and even transform what was shattered.

James has the right of it: *"But the wisdom from above is first of all pure. It is also peace loving, gentle at all times, and willing to yield to others. It is full of mercy and good deeds. It shows no favoritism and is always sincere. And those who are peacemakers will plant seeds of peace and reap a harvest of righteousness."* [James 3:17,18]

We need the Lord's help to apply this to our lives, to seek peace with all who have harmed us in order that our hearts will be blameless and free of pain and shame. Only He can restore our own brokenness and build bridges of reconciliation in all our severed relationships. Amen.

The Miracle of Perseverance

The life of Joseph references the miracle of perseverance. We may consider the fact that we are able to persevere as something either innate or learned, yet the very act of persevering suggests inordinate strength in extraordinary circumstances. Where else can that come from but from the Spirit of God moving within us to accomplish the impossible.

The word perseverance suggests two ideas: preserve and severe and it is as if God is preserving us through severe circumstances. You may already be looking at the situations you are in and thinking that is what my life is like right now: severe circumstances. That is what makes Joseph's experiences such a great lesson in how to receive the miracle of perseverance.

We see him as a young, cocky teenager sporting his fancy colorful coat, confident of his father's love and assured of his important family position as the firstborn son of Jacob's beloved wife Rachel. It's possible that by his favored position he always received the best of everything and was rarely corrected. He was even so arrogant that when his older brothers did something wrong that he'd run to his father tattling about their mischief-making. At this point he certainly didn't understand familial loyalty or the awful price of carrying tales about others. Naturally his brothers hated him. Their dad had repeatedly made it abundantly obvious that they were second best. They saw it when they were returning home to Canaan and their uncle Esau met them with 400 warriors. Jacob placed Rachel and her sons right beside him whereas Leah and her sons were in front and thus more vulnerable to attack. It was those not so subtle signs that showed they didn't hold as great a place in their father's heart.

Thus, when Joseph, probably whistling a happy, contented tune, went looking for his brothers at his father's request and that, unsuspecting any treachery, walked up to them unarmed and unprotected. Probably too late, he caught their glowering expressions, just as they yanked off his fancy coat and tossed him into the waterless pit. The cruel desert sun beat mercilessly upon his head; his throat caked with desert dust and his tummy rumbled its hungry complaints, yet his pitiful cries for help went unheeded. He could hear them just out of reach, laughing and talking, even mocking him while they ate and drank contentedly.

This was not at all what he expected. His dreams revealed a blessed and favored life in which not only his brothers, but even his father and mother would bow before him in reverence. Yet now he was the one bowing, on his knees, in a pit; his voice raspy with thirst as his tongue stuck to the roof of his mouth. 'Oh, God', he thought, 'help me. Get me out of this hole'.

Then he heard the chuff of camels, the rough voices of traders, and he heard the frightening clink of coins just before a rope was thrown down to him. Scrambling up, he undoubtedly thought, 'Thank you, God, for getting me out of that ditch'. But before he could even look around him, calloused hands grabbed his arms and tied them together, securing the other end to the saddle on the camel's back. 'Brothers, what is this? What are you doing? Look the game is over now. You've had your fun. If you let me go, I won't even tell father what you did to me. I'll tell him the bruises are just from a fall down a sand dune'.

But their hard faces told a different story as they spat in the sand. Then with a sneer, they turned away and with an arm wrenching yank, Joseph was pulled away. Mile after dusty mile, he had only the white-hot sand beneath him and the smelly, swaying backside of a camel before him. This was no dream, but a nightmare. He was no longer a favored son, but a worthless slave. He no longer had his fill of tasty figs, olives and bread dipped in oil, but meager scraps. For mile after lonely mile, his mind drifted between what was, to what is, and the terror of what may be. How did he not just drop to his knees and give up? How did he manage to take one step in front of another? How did his heart not break at the horror of what he'd lost? This was the miracle of perseverance. Perhaps he was thinking 'I had a dream. I am to lead my family.' Yet it certainly didn't look like that right now. No doubt his future seemed like a distant mirage, but still he believed the vision, and with that thought he was able to place one foot in front of the other.

Even when he stood on the auction block; even when Potiphar paid the coin for a new household slave, Joseph said 'this is not my permanent place'. That was why when Potiphar's wife tried to lure him into her bed, he could respectfully but firmly turn away from her temptations. He knew she was not the way to God's future. Once again Satan wanted him to trip up, but his feet stood firm. Even when his master believed the false accusation of rape and cast him into prison, he believed this was not his permanent place.

Even there in a dark, dank and dirty prison, he believed the vision. He completed his chores diligently; acted respectfully; showed intelligence and perseverance, when the prison walls could have crushed the life out of him. His faithfulness saw his elevation once again just as he had experienced in Potiphar's house. The warden entrusted him with greater and greater responsibilities and with each one he exceeded all expectations. Why? Because he had a dream. He knew what he was called to do, and as such he could persevere in the most dreadful circumstances.

This placed him before the Pharaoh's baker and cupbearer, two men who also understood sudden and fearful humiliation. One minute in respectable and elevated positions and the next chained to a prison wall. One body-cramped night, their dreams cascaded into bewildering images. They awoke with their hearts seized with alarm and their thoughts rampaging in panic. 'What could these things mean?' they wondered. Joseph immediately noticed their discomfort and asked them what was wrong. 'Our dreams," they cried. They've haunted us and we don't know what they mean.'

"Interpreting dreams is God's business," Joseph replied. "Go ahead

and tell me your dreams." [Genesis 40:8] Joseph had no problem putting his faith before him. Even in this land of multiple gods who were worshipped with horrendous rituals of carnage and debauchery, Joseph let his faith in the one true God be known. Recognizing Joseph's faith-filled confidence, the cupbearer revealed his dream and Joseph, inspired by the Holy Spirit, provided the interpretation: he would be restored to his position. The chief baker was encouraged by this report and excitedly shared his dream, but the interpretation was bleak. Death! Not a word you'd want to give to anyone, even a stranger, but Joseph was obedient and delivered God's message, and the dreams were fulfilled.

Despite his restoration, the cup bearer forgot all about Joseph. Two full years elapsed and still Joseph remained in prison. Did you get that: Two Full Years. Forgotten by men but remembered by God, Joseph persevered. He remained faithful. He continued doing the next thing God told him to do while in the most unpleasant of circumstances. Then at last the time came. Pharaoh lay tossing on his bed. Frightening dreams rolled before him one after the other: fat cows, thin cows, plump stalks, withered stalks. He awoke heavy hearted and frightened. In a land where dreams foretold the future, Pharaoh hungered for understanding. But his wise men and magicians could offer no illumination. At last his cup bearer came forward. 'I know someone', he said, and bravely recounted the story of his prison dream and its interpreter.

Pharaoh didn't hesitate. It didn't matter that Joseph was an imprisoned foreigner, a disgusting Hebrew no less, for the Egyptians held them in contempt. Immediately he called for Joseph, had him washed and properly clothed. When Joseph was at last standing before him, Pharaoh spilled out his problem. Joseph didn't hesitate. Even now, at last breathing the clean air of freedom, he expressed his faith: *"It is beyond my power to do this," Joseph replied. "But God can tell you what it means and set you at ease."* [Genesis 41:16] Pharaoh was undeterred. He recounted the dreams in detail. With startling clarity, the Spirit revealed the interpretation and Joseph explained in detail what God intended to do.

Did Joseph imagine what Pharaoh would say next? Did he know that this would be his moment? Undoubtedly, he knew that it was coming because God had revealed this to him in a dream decades before, but when Pharaoh actually spoke the words: *"Since God has revealed the meaning of the dreams to you, clearly no one else is as intelligent or wise as you are. You will be in charge of my court, and all my people will take orders from you. Only I, sitting on my throne, will have a rank higher than yours."..."I hereby put you in charge of the entire land of Egypt."* [Genesis 41:39-41] undoubtedly a tremor went through Joseph. The moment he'd meet his brothers, the ones who had thrown him in the pit, sold him into slavery, and triggered years of imprisonment was still to come. But it would come. And they would throw themselves to their knees before their brother just as God had foretold.

The miracle of perseverance. Joseph's story encourages us to hold on. What God has said will come to pass. We can't give up. We have to let God do His miraculous work of perseverance in our lives in order to see His glory unfold. Paul understood the miracle of perseverance and wrote to the Romans [15:13]: *"I pray that God, the source of hope, will fill you completely with joy and peace because you trust in him. Then you will overflow with confident hope through the power of the Holy Spirit."* May we also await our miracle of perseverance for God's time of freedom and restoration will come.

The Miracle of Hope

Hope – believing the unexpected is possible. That is what Jochebed believed. Despite a lifetime of slavery; despite marrying someone she loved; bearing his children knowing they, too, would live as slaves, she had hope. How do I know that? Let's look at her story. It opens in Exodus 1 where we learn that centuries after the leadership of Joseph, Egypt had a new and heartless ruler (Exodus 1:8). All that the faithful Joseph had done for Pharaoh and the Egyptian people in averting the famine had mildewed in ancient unread records. The promises and provisions for Israel and his family had long since disappeared. Four hundred years later these events were far distant memories.

The Hebrews, viewed with contempt by the Egyptians even when Joseph was alive, had now become a dangerous element by their sheer strength of numbers. This Pharaoh was not going to take any chances that his enslaved populace would one day turn against them and so to defend, he offended. He put them to bitter labor, forcing them to construct his massive pyramids. When this backbreaking labor didn't crush them, he enforced a new policy of torture: at birth, every boy child would be killed. Only the girl children would be allowed to live – as slaves.

Undeterred, the wise and resourceful midwives, Shiphrah and Puah, devised a plan to save the children, reporting that they couldn't arrive at the birthing early enough to destroy the newborns for the

Hebrew women were too vigorous (Exodus 1:19) These brave midwives willingly faced death and God honored their courage and rewarded them with families of their own. Then Pharaoh instituted another dastardly plan: toss every Hebrew boy into the Nile [Exodus 1:22].

It's at this juncture that we're introduced to the young Levite couple, Amram and Jochebed. Their marriage produced first a girl, then a boy [Exodus 7:7]. The first son was allowed to live, perhaps because he was birthed before the pronouncement that all boy babies were to be drowned in the Nile, but it was her second son that Jochebed feared would be killed. She turned to God for comfort and hope, echoing the words of the Psalmist who would later write: *"When doubts filled my mind, your comfort gave me renewed hope and cheer."* [Psalm 94:19]

She kept her infant son secreted away from the soldiers' prying eyes as long as possible, resolving that *"Lord, where do I put my hope? My only hope is in you."* [Psalm 39:7] But by three months his cooing and crying forced her to do the impossible. Place him in the Nile - yet not unprotected. With the painstaking love that only a mother can give, she carefully crafted a small basket, covering it with pitch to prevent it from taking on water and sinking its precious cargo. Obedient in principle to Pharaoh's demand, she set her love-drenched burden in the Nile, praying fervently that the basket would stay afloat and that the snapping, ever-hungry crocodiles would seal their tooth-filled jaws and not shatter her miniature, wave tossed houseboat. Breath frozen in her chest, she sent her daughter, Miriam, to watch over her baby brother and scamper after the basket as it meandered with the current.

Horrified, Miriam watched as her tiny brother, cradled in his makeshift crib, neared the palace. And then to make matters worse, a royal entourage of women stepped lightly toward the edge of the river, Pharaoh's daughter amongst them. Miriam would know nothing of the character of this woman; she wouldn't know if she would leave the baby to its fate or submerge it herself to fulfill her father's command. Yet with whispered prayers for mercy, Miriam saw the woman startle at the sound of a baby's cry, draw the basket near and tentatively lift its lid and then watched as the woman's face softened into a gentle smile.

Taken by the beauty and innocence of this little one's face, the princess cooed softly at the wiggling bundle. Quick witted like her mother, Miriam ran forward: *"Should I go and find one of the Hebrew women to nurse the baby for you?" she asked.* [Exodus 2:7]

And that is how Jochebed was rewarded for her ingenuity. Not only was Moses saved from drowning, but he was guaranteed the loving arms of his mother to raise him; the sweetness of her breast milk to nurture him; the tenderness of her spiritual teachings to instill his cultural heritage. During his formative years, this little boy would receive instruction from his mother; be lullabied to sleep with her songs; and soothed by her comfort when the scrapes of toddlerhood wounded him. Through these events, we see God fulfilling the words of Proverbs 10:28 that *"the hopes of the godly result in happiness"*. Only when he was weaned would Jochebed return him to Pharaoh's daughter, who would raise him in the Egyptian palace. By these miraculous turn of events, Moses would become part of the royal family, receive the privileges and education of nobility, and secure a favored position in Pharaoh's court.

Do you see the miracle of hope in this story? Here was a slave woman, who knew well the cruelty of the Egyptian taskmasters, the viciousness of Pharaoh's hateful decrees, yet would willingly bear a child, a son no less, into such a formidable and frightening world. It is the miracle of hope that would believe that her child would live; that her child was destined for greater things than what she'd known or seen; that God had better plans for this little one than even she could imagine. She believed with the prophet Jeremiah: *"There is hope for your future," says the Lord. "Your children will come again to their own land."* [Jeremiah 31:17]. This is the miracle of hope.

It is again the miracle of hope that believed that she had secured the co-operation of the other women in her community – first the midwives who would profess they could not reach her in time to prevent her birthing a live male child. Then the other women who shared her secret and knew that Jochebed had hidden an infant in her home and secretly cared for him all those weeks. For all of them, hope blossomed that this little one must be saved; his life protected and preserved for God's holy plan. Not only this, it is the miracle of hope that brought forth the plan to save her child. Crafting a special river-resistant cradle that he might float in freedom and yes even safety. In her cunning, she used the very plans of evil – abandoning her helpless infant to the waters of death – to turn them into salvation – lowering him not into the sacred waters but on top of them that they might carry him to safety.

Willingly Jochebed faced her fears, believing not in what could be seen with the human eye, but what could be seen with the spiritual one, that God had called this child from the sanctuary of her womb and would Himself provide another sanctuary to raise him into manhood. And so, she set the child upon the waters, but did not leave him to his fate. She called her daughter, the youngster she'd raised with the wisdom born of the ages, and instructed her to watch over her baby brother, to ensure that the waters carried him to refuge and not ruin.

She could never have foreseen or prepared for what happened. She could not have given her daughter instructions on how to save her brother. This was merely the quick thinking of a young girl who saw an opportunity and leaped on it. Praying and longing for the miracle of hope, Miriam grasped with both hands and a bold mouth the moment when it arrived. It was like a rainbow wrapped in iridescent colors, following the deluge of a storm, promising a future and a hope, and Miriam reached out and grabbed it, offering the baby's own mother as a nursemaid.

Thus, with the miracle of hope blossoming in Jochabed's heart she thought, 'Good will come from this. My baby will yet live and breathe freedom greater than I shall ever know.' And so day after day, Jochebed placed her tiny baby to her breast; watched in wonder as his brown eyes sparkled with love. Like Hannah [1 Samuel 1], Jochebed was blessed with the opportunity of raising her child before releasing him to be reared by another. Still the miracle of hope said that these years would establish this little one's footsteps and they would lead him to the presence and purpose of God.

It seems likely that Jochebed did not live to see her son defend his beleaguered people. Certainly, she'd be gone before he would ever return to stand before Pharaoh and challenge him to free his people.

Yet throughout her days, she lived with the miracle of hope dwelling in her bosom, believing that what her eye could not see; nor her ears could hear, God would bring to pass [1 Corinthians 2:9]. Thus, through Jochebed's life, we witness the miracle of hope. Through her, we see Hebrews 11:1,2: *"Faith is the confidence that what we hope for will actually happen; it gives us assurance about things we cannot see. Through their faith, the people in the days of old earned a good reputation."*

Thus, despite our circumstances, our current reality, may we live in the miracle of hope, and see with faith-filled eyes the deliverance that God has planned for us.

The Miracle of God's Call

Do you remember the first time you realized God was calling you? I don't mean into ministry or missions, but when you heard God calling you to Himself. It was remarkable, wasn't it? A moment none of us ever forgets when we realize that the God of the Universe is personally reaching out to us. Think about that moment as we consider how Moses must have felt.

The Word tells us in Exodus 2 that he was remarkably saved when his ingenious mom crafted a special water-resistant basket for him and placed him in the Nile River. Then God stirred the current and directed that tiny houseboat right next to the palace, knowing that Pharaoh's compassionate daughter would be coming to bathe, and would take one peak at this little tike and want him for her child. With supernatural insight, she even allowed Moses' own mother to care for him until he was weaned, providing him with his spiritual roots and cultural identity.

Then Moses was brought to the palace to be raised in wealth and splendor with the most advanced tutors guiding him in the world's knowledge. Yet still his spiritual foundation remained firmly intact for when he became an adult, he rescued an oppressed brother. This overzealous action forced him to flee the palace and begin his long and fateful journey that led him to Jethro, a Midian priest. Knowing his former palace life was lost to him, Moses remained and created a young family of his own with his new wife Zipporah, Jethro's daughter. Seemingly in the blink of an eye, he went from wealthy stepson to poor shepherd and spent the next four decades in this wasteland, watching over sheep. Then one day he witnessed an incredible sight, a bush consumed in flames, but instead of turning to ash it remained vibrant with life. Curiosity peaked, Moses turned aside to witness how the impossible was possible. It was then God called to him.

Would his years in the desert make him immune to the amazing, indifferent to the miraculous? Had the Wow gone out of him, making him yawn at the impossible. God needed to know if Moses was still impressed with the wondrous. Moses turned, he looked, he listened. Is it likely Moses recognized the voice of God? Perhaps not, but still he immediately answered: *"Here I am!"* [Exodus 3:4] He wanted to be found and listened carefully as God explained who He was and affirmed His long-standing relationship with His people [Exodus 3:6].

Moses, contrite before a holy God, bowed in worship, feeling the shame and remorse of his youthful actions: the soldier's murder and the abandonment of his family and responsibilities. Then God called Moses away from his past failures to his future calling: Free the people. He'd heard their cry, knew their suffering, and chose to rescue them from to deliver them to [Exodus 3:7-10]. What does this passage in Exodus 3 tell us? Firstly, God hears our cry. It may seem as if He isn't listening or doing anything to help, but He's always active, never passive, always moving, never stagnant, always caring, never careless. God knows what's happening in our lives and is planning something too marvelous to imagine.

God explained His plans and then involved Moses in the miracle. Look – He says. Just like He needed Moses to look at the burning bush, Moses had to listen to His call. 'Look! I've heard and seen the distress of My people. I've let you spend forty years in the wilderness to prepare you for what I'll have you do. You're no longer some hot-headed youngster that thinks he can solve the problems of the world with his fists. You are a matured adult, who has followed directions, fathered sons, and guided sheep. All of this was to prepare you for the work ahead.'

Moses didn't feel those wilderness years had been long enough or sharp enough to make him the man God thought he could be. He didn't think he could stand before Pharaoh again. It'd been too many years since he'd walked with royalty. How could he ever lead people when he'd only guided sheep? God answered: *"I will be with you."* And to reassure Moses, He told him that he'd return to this very spot: *"And this is your sign that I am the one who has sent you: When you have brought the people out of Egypt, you will worship God at this very mountain."* [Exodus 3:12] Still Moses' had more fear than faith and protested again: *"If I go to the people of Israel and tell them, 'The God of your ancestors has sent me to you,' they will ask me, 'What is his name?' Then what should I tell them?"* [Exodus 3:13]

Remember he hadn't spoken to God before; he wasn't sure he really knew who was calling his name. 'Who are you?' he was saying. God wasn't daunted by Moses' doubt and so He patiently explained: *"I AM WHO I AM. Say this to the people of Israel: I AM has sent me to you."* God also said to Moses, *"Say this to the people of Israel: Yahweh, the God of your ancestors—the God of Abraham, the God of Isaac, and the God of Jacob—has sent me to you. This is my eternal name, my name to remember for all generations".* [Exodus 3:14,15]

I am always and forever. I am all there is and ever will be. With the statement: "I AM" God explained: 'I am everything and all in all. You need never look again for Creator, Protector, Deliverer, Friend'. Then God gave him specific directions and reassured him that the elders would receive his leadership, but Pharaoh would not. It would take God's mighty hand to deliver them. Despite these assurances, Moses was still afraid.

As if the burning bush wasn't enough, God showed him another miracle: transforming his shepherd's staff into a snake. Interesting isn't it, that he would take the tool that Moses had used to guide his sheep and turn it into a fearsome reptile. In the same way God can change the simple, Moses, into the powerful, a deliverer, to accomplish His purposes. Then He gave him the astonishing direction to grab hold of the snake. Anyone that handles snakes knows you never want to pick them up by the tail as they can quickly flick around and bite you.

But this was another trust exercise, just like the next one when God turned his healthy hand into a leprous one and then back to healthy one. Perhaps God was suggesting, 'Your life is in my hands. Trust me with it.'

Still Moses wasn't convinced. Despite all he'd just seen, he doubted: 'You, God, can do all of that, but me, I'm nothing. I can't even talk right anymore. Surely You've got the wrong man'. But God's calling was irrevocable. He knew Moses could do it: *"Who makes a person's mouth? Who decides whether people speak or do not speak, hear or do not hear, see or do not see? Is it not I, the LORD? Now go! I will be with you as you speak, and I will instruct you in what to say."* [Exodus 4:11]

Dear, doubting Moses. Does he sound like us? With all that God said, did, promised, still Moses doubted, yet God made provision for Moses' fear, sending his brother Aaron to him as a spokesman and empowering his shepherd's staff to become a tool of deliverance. It's as if God was saying: 'Take all I've given you Moses: My Words, My promise, My presence, even your brother and staff. Take all of this and go. Fulfill your calling.'

God is saying the same to each of us today. 'I have called you from whatever desert you are in; from whatever place of insignificance you think you are at'. Then He soaks us with His Word, His promise, His Presence. He gives us brothers and sisters in the Lord to help us, and tools to aid us in our ministry. Whatever doubts or fears we have, we can lay them aside. For God is with us; His Spirit fills us; and His gifts and fruits empower us to go forth in victory. Let this be our day of redemption. Our day of miracles. This is our day to do the amazing and impossible with Jesus.

Mayhem and Miracles

Moses doubted that he had the character or qualities necessary to approach Pharaoh, but there he was plodding through the desert on his way back to Egypt. His wife, children and his eloquent brother beside him. Why the reluctance? You may recall that God needed to convince Moses that he was the man for the job, and it took quite a bit of convincing. Words were not enough. He had to show him by turning the staff into a snake, his healthy hand into a diseased one, and even water into blood. Still I wonder if Moses had a residual of doubt clinging to him. After all, hadn't God said that, despite the numerous wonders, Pharaoh would still refuse to let the Israelites go? Nonetheless, Moses pressed on until he was face to face with Pharaoh, the arrogant, irate ruler who mocked his petition [Exodus 5:2].

Sounds like some of our bosses or family members, doesn't it, when we try to tell them about God? Even the warning about horrible plagues wouldn't soften Pharaoh's stone heart. He didn't believe, let alone care what this Hebrew God could do. 'Get back to work. And don't bother me with this foolishness any more. Time is money.' Unfortunately, Moses and Aaron's visit caused severe consequences: less straw, more bricks. The overworked slaves were even accused of laziness. When the exhausted slaves were unable to keep up, they were beaten for their failure to perform. They complained bitterly to Moses: "*May the LORD judge and punish you for making us stink before Pharaoh and his officials. You have put a sword into their hands, an excuse to kill us!"* [Exodus 5:21]

What a miserable situation all around. What could Moses do, but appeal to God who'd sent him there in the first place: *"Why have you brought all this trouble on your own people, Lord? Why did you send me? Ever since I came to Pharaoh as your spokesman, he has been even more brutal to your people. And you have done nothing to rescue them!"* [Exodus 5:22,23]

Does any of this ring true for you? Have you ever stumbled upon catastrophe when you've tried to follow the Lord? Stepped into one disaster after another when you've tried to live faithfully. I remember a time when we needed a second car and found a great looking model for a ridiculously low price. Yes, it was decades old and when I drove it, it rattled like a baby's toy, but my husband and I prayed and felt the Lord told us to buy it. Of course, it needed loads of repairs that cost us three times what we'd initially paid for the car. It was an irreparable clunker. To this day, we're not sure what God was trying to teach us. It was a lesson in obedience even if the outcome wasn't what we imagined.

I'm sure Moses must have felt that way, too, but God was undaunted by the circumstances. He knew the end result: His people's freedom and He told Moses: *"Now you will see what I will do to Pharaoh. When he feels the force of my strong hand, he will let the people go. In fact, he will force them to leave his land!"* [Exodus 6:1] God reminds Moses: 'I made a covenant with My people centuries ago that they would have the land of Canaan. This is the moment of fulfillment. Get ready.' Can you almost sense the tingle of excitement; the crackle of anticipation that something wondrous was about to happen? Moses must have felt it for he returned to Pharaoh, raised the staff and commenced the wonders.

But it started almost as a fizzle and a pop. The staff turning into a snake brought a yawn from Pharaoh as his magicians duplicated the miracle. It was the same with the water to blood, perhaps not on the same grand scale and certainly not the waters of their beloved Nile, but through their devilish arts Pharaoh's conjurers replicated the deed.

They even matched the invasion of frogs, yet they couldn't eradicate the nasty little ribbetters. But from here on Pharaoh's magicians couldn't equal God's power, and it was a tiny gnat that made the difference and caused the astonished magicians to declare: *"This is the finger of God!"* [Exodus 8:19]

Have you ever thought about these plagues? Can you imagine digging gnats out of your ears and eyes and spitting gnats off your tongue every time you tried to open your mouth? Not a pleasant experience. Yet still Pharaoh refused to listen. Next it was flies – dirty little buzzing beasts. Furthermore, the land of Goshen, the region of the Israelites would be free of the pests. God was showing a distinct difference between His people and Pharaoh's [Exodus 8:22,23].

In exasperation, Pharaoh relented and released them to make their sacrifices, if Moses would free them from this disgusting plague. Yet no sooner had the buzzing ceased than Pharaoh changed his mind, refusing to let them go. You can almost hear God sighing at Pharaoh's stubbornness. Then with a flick of His finger, all the Egyptian livestock fell over dead – every cow, sheep, camel, donkey, and goat – but Pharaoh didn't even flinch. After all, he had all the wealth and power he needed.

Even when the boils came, afflicting all the Egyptian's including the magicians with their fiery torment, Pharaoh stuck his nose arrogantly in the air. Hail followed, but before it fell, Moses warned Pharaoh to call the people indoors for their safety. Those who doubted and didn't, died as the rocks of ice plummeted to earth. At last, Pharaoh appeared genuinely repentant: *"I have sinned,"* he confessed. *"The LORD is the righteous one, and my people and I are wrong. Please beg the LORD to end this terrifying thunder and hail. We've had enough. I will let you go."* [Exodus 9:27,28] Yet, once again as soon as the skies cleared, Pharaoh turned a stubborn heart toward the merciful face of God.

The Lord prefaced His next miracle with this word: 'I'm doing this for three reasons: to display my miraculous signs among the Egyptians; to testify to your children and grandchildren of my wonders against the Egyptians; to show you that I am the LORD.' Then the locusts came, devouring the remaining wheat crops that the hail had not destroyed.

Deep darkness came next, so thick and complete that for three days the Egyptians couldn't move. Only the Israelites had light, clearly illustrating that God Himself is the Light of the world. Finally, Pharaoh had enough. In despair and disgust he commanded: *"Go and worship the LORD." "But leave your flocks and herds here. You may even take your little ones with you."* [Exodus 10:24]

Yet how would they sacrifice without their herds. Pharaoh's offer was insufficient, but when Moses explained this, Pharaoh erupted in anger. He was the leader; he didn't negotiate; he commanded, and people obeyed. *"Get out of here!" Pharaoh shouted at Moses. "I'm warning you. Never come back to see me again! The day you see my face, you will die!"* Moses wasn't worried. God was on his side. *"Very well,"* Moses replied. *"I will never see your face again."* [Exodus 10:28,29]

The plagues had reached a crescendo. The final moment had come. Soon the enslaved would be free; the oppressed liberated. But God had to prepare His people first. For centuries they'd been under the thumb of the Egyptians; they'd lost sight of their service and sacrifice to God. He needed to re-invigorate the practice, but also refine it for future generations. Moreover, He needed to illuminate the people's heart on the perfect sacrifice to come. His eyes were already cast across the centuries to a hill where the blood of His only Son would be shed to set all captives free once, forever. Thus, He instructed them to prepare an unblemished sacrifice, sweep its blood across their doorposts for then the angel of death would pass over their household.

That evening the silence was broken by the sound of wailing, fathers and mothers sobbing for the children who, unprotected by the sacrifice, succumbed to the Deadly Visitor. Even bold, brash Pharaoh crumpled in grief, weeping for his firstborn son dead in his arms. Before morning even dawned, Pharaoh called Moses and Aaron and bellowed: *"Get out!" "Leave my people—and take the rest of the Israelites with you! Go and worship the LORD as you have requested. Take your flocks and herds, as you said, and be gone. Go, but bless me as you leave."* [Exodus 12:31,32] At last, Israel was free.

Although the oppression had been excruciating, the miracles were astounding. The plagues, which crushed every Egyptian god to dust, stands as a testimony in their minds -and ours – as to God's magnificence. We must ask ourselves where we are at in this story? Trying to make bricks without straw, feeling the weight of the whip, watching the wonders unfold, or packing our bags for freedom. Wherever we are at in this journey, may we take the hand of God, walk with courage and faithfulness and see the glories ahead.

Calm in the Chaos

Have you ever thought of your life's journey? Sometimes there have been smooth, paved roads; other times there have been detours; popped tires; empty gas tanks; all sorts of things to slow you down. Sometimes even a minor bump in the road has had major consequences. Certainly, the journey of Moses and the Israelites were beset with difficulties. They'd just endured weeks of mind-boggling plagues which left their Egyptian masters angry and miserable. No one wants to work for a cranky boss, especially if he or she blames you for their problems. Then the unexpected. A special meal, a night of eerie calm, then suddenly a piercing wail followed by the shouts: 'Get dressed, gather your things and get out'.

After 430 years of captivity, to the very day, they were heading to freedom. Over a half million men along with their families started out from Egypt. Their initial 120-mile trek from Ramses towards Succoth was arduous. It may not seem far by car but imagine if you have pregnant women and tiny babes along with rickety carts crammed with your meager belongings and then flighty sheep and goats skittering nervously here and there. What a nightmare? And in the darkness no less. Then when day comes, you're still trudging over desert. You're hot, tired, thirsty, hungry. Suddenly your love for freedom may not taste so sweet.

Added to this was the fact that the map God gave you seemed

off-kilter. We are told: *"When Pharaoh finally let the people go, God did not lead them along the main road that runs through Philistine territory, even though that was the shortest route to the Promised Land. God said, "If the people are faced with a battle, they might change their minds and return to Egypt." So God led them in a roundabout way through the wilderness toward the Red Sea. Thus the Israelites left Egypt like an army ready for battle."* [Exodus 13:17,18]

Those directions would definitely put your teeth on edge, knowing that you had to be ever vigilant for battle. After all, despite the blood, gnats, flies, cattle, disease, and darkness, Pharaoh still refused to let his slaves go. Then his first-born son dies. He was enraged at the loss and sought revenge. These were tense moments. But unlike the plagues when they could only see the effect of God's power, now the Children of Israel actually saw His presence with them. *"The LORD went ahead of them. He guided them during the day with a pillar of cloud, and he provided light at night with a pillar of fire. This allowed them to travel by day or by night."* [Exodus 13:21] Day and night God's presence went before them, guiding their way, reassuring them that they weren't alone; reminding them He was always with them. Can you imagine the peace they must have felt – after all the years of trauma?

Then something unusual happened. They were told to retrace their steps, to turn back and camp by the shore. Murmurs of discontent built until they were noticeable grumbles and then loud angry voices. Rumors circulated that Pharaoh and his battle-hardened soldiers were coming after them. Worse still, they felt trapped and in horror watched as a massive dust cloud barreled toward them with the Egyptian soldiers at its center. Like any of us, the Israelites panicked. They screamed at Moses: 'We survived years of captivity, the gruesome plagues, now we face sword wielding soldiers who hate us. You've led us out here to die'. Moses raised his hands to quiet their shouts. *"Don't be afraid. Just stand still and watch the LORD rescue you today. The Egyptians you see today will never be seen again. The LORD himself will fight for you. Just stay calm."* [Exodus 14:13,14]

Have you ever faced a battle and God gave you such a word of assurance? How did you feel? Did your pounding heart calm? Did your agitation cease? Perhaps you shook your head and wondered, 'But how God. They are too strong, too powerful; the situation is too dark and horrible'.

Moses must have been feeling that way too, for he cried out to God for help. Immediately, God demanded action, instructing Moses to pick up his staff and thrust it toward the waters [Exodus 14:15-18]. Are you standing still as your enemy snorts and rants and raves in front of you? Maybe you need to "get moving". Face the barrier and see God's hand part it like water. After all it isn't about us or our problems; it's about God's glory. It certainly doesn't mean God doesn't care about the cries of His people, or that He doesn't care about our needs. He does! It just means that in the bigger picture, He knows He's going to deliver us, and that through our deliverance, others will see the glory of God. How wonderful is that!

But our story isn't over yet. God divinely protected them in a supernatural way. The day time cloud settled before them shielding them from the stampeding army and, as the sun set, it transformed into an impenetrable pillar of fire, preventing the Egyptians from coming any closer to the helpless Israelites. Still God wasn't finished yet. Then He had Moses raise his staff over the sea, that Holy Spirit anointed staff that had accomplished so many miracles. The Israelites felt the wind pick up until it was blowing fiercely. People by the shore could see the waves swirl in ever-quickening eddies, until to their jaw-dropping amazement, the waters parted revealing the dry sea bed as a ribbon-like highway before them. Moses turned to the frightened people and waved them onward. Mountains of waves walled them in on either side. Schools of fish, huge whales, vicious sharks all swam to the edges of the clear wall of water. The Israelites rushed forward, driving their herds, carrying their children, supporting their elderly, together they raced ahead until they stepped onto freedom's shore.

Then the thought struck them – if they got through this miraculous highway, couldn't their enemy as well. They looked back and to their horror they saw that the impenetrable firewall had lifted allowing the soldiers to charge toward them. Then something amazing happened. Suddenly, the sea bed became slushy with water and the chariot wheels careened to a stop. In the confusion, the horses reared. Panic seized these battle-hardened men. Too late they realized what was happening: *"Let's get out of here—away from these Israelites!" the Egyptians shouted. "The LORD is fighting for them against Egypt!"* [Exodus 14:25]

They saw Moses on the far shore, with that accursed staff in his hand, raised high overhead. In terror they watched as he swung it downward. They heard an ominous rumble moments before tons of water battered them into the seabed. Their enemy was destroyed. A whoop of joy could be heard for miles around. Free at last. Some astute ones threw themselves to their knees and praised the God of heaven and earth for His mighty power. Others pounded Moses on his back and shouted thanks to God. After generations of oppression, poverty and hard labor, the children of Israel were free at last.

God used a method so radical, so unforgettable that it became a tale told across continents and centuries. Whether you've been a believer for a long or a short time, you would have heard this story. Perhaps you've asked God to part the waters for you as well. Asked Him to set you free from hardships and sufferings. Maybe you needed to hear this story again today. You needed to be reminded of what God did for His people at their desperate hour. You needed to know that God can do all things at all times no matter how great or powerful your enemy or how desperate your situation may seem.

What did Moses say again: *"Don't be afraid. Just stand still and watch the LORD rescue you today. The enemy you see today will never be seen again. The LORD himself will fight for you. Just stay calm."* [Exodus 14:13,14]

Be encouraged, Beloved. This word is for you. Don't be afraid. Just stay calm. Watch and see what our Lord will do. He is still our miracle maker.

Celebrations and Sins

The miracle of the Red Sea is a story that we can hear over and over again. We all feel like we've faced an impossible situation with no apparent way out and then suddenly a door opens, and we can walk through into something new, something beautiful, something better. That's how our God works.

But we can't stop our story here for it is far from over. The children of Israel have just witnessed an unprecedented miracle. The impossible made possible. It took the Red Sea for them to find their faith. Years of captivity and the daily cruelty of slavery had turned their hearts to stone. It had been so long since they'd seen the light of day, they couldn't quite believe that it'd come. Then they endured the desperate trek across the desert only to face the impassable waters of the Red Sea. All of this begged the question: 'Where to go from here?' They'd already backtracked to make it to this place. Then to their horror they saw the ominous dust cloud of the Egyptian army barreling toward them. The hope that had flickered in their hearts fizzled out. They were trapped with nowhere to go.

But then God – the power of those three little words. The waves stood up allowing thousands of people to walk to freedom. It stirs our hearts just to think of it as it did the Israelites. Immediately, Moses led them in worship: an inspired song that declared: *"I will sing to the LORD, for he has triumphed gloriously; he has hurled both horse and rider into the sea. The* LORD *is my strength and my song; he has given me victory. This is my God, and I will praise him—my father's God, and I will exalt him!"* [Exodus 15:1,2]

His sister Miriam led the women in dance beside him, with tambourines jangling out a victory beat. It was a euphoric moment when all the tension of slavery slipped away, the stifling fear of death disappeared. Before them lay incredible possibilities. Where to begin?

Yet their journey wasn't over. They couldn't remain on the shores of the Red Sea, but where could they go. The desert stretched before them and in just three days, their tongues stuck to the roof of their mouths. The blazing sun blinded them during the day and the chill of night cramped their tired muscles. 'Hey,' they probably thought, 'this wasn't supposed to happen.' 'We were supposed to be headed into a land of milk and honey. What are we doing here? Why are we in the desert, parched with thirst?' Hadn't God given them victory? Hadn't He cast their enemies into the sea? Why were they facing these problems?

Have you asked these questions? You just got this great job? Began this wonderful relationship and suddenly things don't look that good. Your initial moments of joy have evaporated with the cold facts of reality. Your testimony of praise has stuttered into silence.

That's exactly how the Israelites reacted as they grumbled for water. Immediately, God showed Moses what to do and he grabbed just the right branch and heaved it into the water, making the stream not only drinkable but refreshing. Do the people shout out another song of deliverance after they satisfy their thirst? Unfortunately, no. Scripture says nothing about their gratitude, but it does about the lessons God is trying to teach them *"If you will ... then I will"*. [Exodus 15:25,26] It seemed to be a refrain that God spoke to them repeatedly.

Yet they don't appear to listen. Less than a month after leaving Egypt, they complained again. The provisions they'd packed were dry and moldy; they could no longer forage for enough food to satisfy the mobile mob and so they grumbled again [Exodus 16:3]. Listen to what they had to say: *"If only the* LORD *had killed us back in Egypt,"* they moaned. *"There we sat around pots filled with meat and ate all the bread we wanted. But now you have brought us into this wilderness to starve us all to death.*"

Clearly the desert sun had melted their brains or short circuited their memories. They sat around pots of meat in Egypt? Ate their fill of bread? What slaves do you know had that kind of luxurious life? They certainly remembered a very different existence from the reality they endured. Nevertheless, God didn't argue with them; He didn't show them their foolishness, but instead granted them mercy, raining down food from heaven. Despite their grumbling, God set a divine table with not only adequate but delicious provisions. Provisions that would arrive daily for the next forty years [Exodus 16:35].

Did you know God's provision, "manna", means "What is it?", a word equaling their constant questioning of God. Even the name suggests the uncertainty of their hearts. They didn't name it: 'Thank you, Lord' or 'I'm grateful, Father'. No, they named it after their hesitation, to signify their doubt and distrust in the I AM who loved them and provided for them.

I hope this doesn't sound familiar. That when God provides our daily sustenance, we don't ask 'Why this, Lord." "Do I have to eat this again, God? Can't you let me eat …?' And fill in our favorite meal. None of us want to get caught in or mired by the sin of ingratitude, but perhaps we all have to take ownership of it.

The Israelites certainly struggled with it. At their next campsite, despite God's amazing banquet, they became even more demanding. *"Give us water to drink!"* [Exodus 17:2] Where was their humility, their gratefulness? Instead they prickled with attitude. It was at this point that Moses was overwhelmed by their constant complaints. Over 600,000 voices all muttering and grumbling in unison could not help but grate, and so Moses cried out to God: *"What should I do with these people? They are ready to stone me!"* [Exodus 17:4]

God understood his dilemma. After all, He'd been hearing it for thousands of years, countless voices across generations all moaning their grievances to Him despite His goodness and mercy. Thus, He instructed Moses to strike the rock [Exodus 17:5,6]. Moses may not have realized it at the time, but it was a life-changing moment for him, even more climatic than the burning bush, for it determined his future. Pressed to the wall by the cacophony of griping people, his reaction sealed his fate. We read: *"Moses named the place Massah (which means "test") and Meribah (which means "arguing") because the people of Israel argued with Moses and tested the LORD by saying, "Is the LORD here with us or not."* [Exodus 17:7]

What was God's test of the people: 'Will you listen to My voice and obey Me?' It was a test of faithfulness [Exodus 15], and the people of Israel failed the test. The Apostle Paul writes about such a test in his second letter to the Corinthians. *"Examine yourselves to see if your faith is genuine. Test yourselves. Surely you know that Jesus Christ is among you; if not, you have failed the test of genuine faith."* [2 Corinthians 13:5]

We need to ask ourselves the question: Are we grateful or grumbling? Are we thankful for the myriad of things that God does for us every day? And yes Beloved no matter what situation you are in or how trying your circumstances, God is still accomplishing miracles for us every single day. After all we're taking our next breath, aren't we? Are we able to say that we're thankful for what God has done?

What about Moses? He'd faced the incensed Pharaoh and now the bad-tempered Israelites all in his efforts to serve God. He'd reached the end of his patience and, despite having seen His glory, he reacted in the flesh. God tells him: *"When the people of Israel rebelled, you failed to demonstrate my holiness to them at the waters."* [Numbers 27:14; Deuteronomy 32:51] The portion in Exodus 17 suggests all is well. Moses struck the rock as God instructed and the water gushed out. But God knew differently. There was no victory dance, no song of praise, just smashing the rock with a stick.

Moses struck it in anger for their grumbling, not in glory for God's greatness. His enraged reaction cost him entry into the Promised Land. Why you ask? When he'd endured so much, why did he have to pay such a great price for one small act of disobedience. Because he trampled on the holiness of God. Didn't God speak to him about this from the burning bush [Exodus 3:5]? God had given him so much, should He not expect respect. Jesus explained: *"When someone has been given much, much will be required in return; and when someone has been entrusted with much, even more will be required."* [Luke 12:48]

Thus, we must ask ourselves some difficult questions: What are we grumbling about? The type or absence of God's Provision? Our circumstances? Our spiritual leader? Does our griping have eternal consequences for them? Can we say that we: Express gratitude. Pass the test of Faith. Support our spiritual leader so they can enter the Promised Land with us. Let's learn our lessons well to rejoice together in glory.

The Miracle of Godly Counsel

After their miraculous deliverance, the Israelites experienced God's supernatural interventions time and again: refreshing water from the rock, tasty quail from the skies; honey-flavored pastry from the ground. His provisions were creatively endless, and His works became known throughout the region. Even Moses' father-in-law Jethro, a Midianite priest, heard about them and believed it was time for Moses to be reunited with his wife and sons. Moses had spent forty years with this man and had married his daughter. He trusted his counsel and welcomed him with great enthusiasm. Here was someone he could share his triumphs and frustrations with, the highs and lows of this exhausting journey [Exodus 18:7-9]. We all need a Jethro in our lives to encourage us and provide us with godly insights, and Moses was no exception, especially with all the grumbling he'd listened to and skirmishes he'd mediated.

It was after watching Moses tirelessly advocate people's disputes from dawn to dark that Jethro intervened. 'You can't keep doing this', he said. 'Such a demanding schedule will physically, spiritually and emotionally wear you out'. He followed it up with a recommendation that would relieve Moses of the minute disagreements that he'd faced throughout the day, enabling him instead to attend to people's spiritual instruction and mediation [Exodus 18:19-23].

Jethro's advice: establish a structure of leadership that appoints godly individuals to attend minor disputes. His first requirement was character. The individuals selected need to be *"capable, honest men who fear God and hate bribes"* [Exodus 18:21]. Capable suggests a person who has the specific skills needed to fulfill their responsibilities. The wife of noble character found in Proverbs 31 has such qualities as does the prophet Daniel [Daniel 6:3], enabling them to administer households and kingdoms with precision and finesse. Honesty is, of course, another significant quality as it ensures that the skills are rendered with fairness and accuracy as Proverbs 11:3,5 illustrates. This quality also spills into the area of resisting bribes for an honest person will not accept improper or excessive payment for services promised or rendered.

Jethro then recommended a cascading structure of leadership from those overseeing 1000, to 100, to 50 to 10. The person assigned to each area of oversight must have skills incumbent with those responsibilities, for leading ten people is far different from leading one thousand. Undoubtedly Moses understood this when God took him from leading a flock of sheep to a throng of people.

Jethro's wisdom in designing this process of delegation has been successfully implemented by governments, church councils, and community leaders for generations. This form of team work is inspirational and effective for none of us can or should do it alone. Paul explained that the Body of Christ is made up of many parts but that each are necessary and effective for the building up of one another and the expansion of the kingdom of God [1 Corinthians 12:12-31].

Excellent advice, isn't it? We have the opportunity of working together to accomplish what God wants us to do – and we'll never get out of the desert and into His Promised Land without it.

What godly counsellors has God placed in your life over the years? What have they told you to develop in order to become the person that God wants you to be? Peter told his flock to: *"Supplement your faith with a generous provision of moral excellence"* [2 Peter 1:5]. He then intertwined six more qualities: knowledge, self-control, patience, godliness, brotherly affection and love which all work together to help people grow and be more effective [2 Peter 1:8].

Have you been as enthusiastic to receive their counsel as Moses was to receive Jethro's? Have you found their wisdom and insights effective in relieving the pressures you face? When the Holy Spirit places godly people in our lives it's to assist us in dealing with the stresses and uncertainties of life, to implement solutions to thorny relational and at times financial problems. What would have happened if Moses had ignored Jethro's counsel? Could he have continued to manage his burdens on his own. Unlikely. And burn out is something none of us wish to face. Proverbs 20:18 supports this, stating: *"Plans succeed through good counsel; don't go to war without wise advice."*

Yet we must be careful of the counselors we seek? Remember Rehoboam, son of Solomon. He was selected to rule after Solomon's death but unlike his father, he didn't seek the wise counselors who'd advised Solomon, those who had a lifetime of experience in overseeing the kingdom. Rather he chose young men like himself, rash, bold and power-hungry, who wanted others to see their greatness. They cared little for the needs of the people, having lived in luxury and afforded reverence for their wealth and position. Thus, when the people came requesting relief from the decades of heavy taxation imposed by Solomon, they advised maliciousness not mercy [1 Kings 12]. The results were catastrophic. The people rejected Rehoboam's leadership and separated from the kingdom. The hard-fought unity amongst the twelve tribes of Israel was severed in an instant, leaving only the tribe of Judah faithful to Rehoboam.

How do we find good counselors? Proverbs instructs us to look to our parents [6:20-22] and as their instruction is the first we receive and undoubtedly lasts the longest, one can understand why this advice. However, not everyone is blessed with godly parents to lead them closer to Christ, yet we can learn from both their good and bad choices to determine the wisest decisions to make.

Psalm 37:30,31 indicates that we should seek advice from those who are committed to following God's ways, stating: *"the godly offer good counsel; they teach right from wrong. They have made God's laws their own, so they will never slip from his path."* The wisdom book of Proverbs also recommends our friends as a source of godly advice indicating that their sincere interest in what's best for us makes their counsel like fragrant perfume [Proverbs 27:9]. Best of all, however, is Christ Himself, our Wise Counselor [Isaiah 9:6] and Paul recommends that we *"let the message about Christ, in all its richness, fill our lives. Teach and counsel each other with all the wisdom he gives."* [Colossians 3:16]

Receiving the wisdom of godly counselors is without a doubt a miracle of God's intervention, arriving at a perfect point in our lives. Jethro arrived on Moses' doorstep only eight weeks after Moses left Egypt. Jesus knew when to send him and what leadership directions he needed to give. Could Moses possibly have guided this unruly mob for another forty years without Jethro's instructions? Probably not. Even so we need to gratefully receive the counsel offered by godly advisors who provide insights and solutions which help us navigate the crevices of our life's journey. Who fits this role in your life? What have they advised you? How can you put their wise advice into practice today?

The Miracle of God's Counsel

Call to me and I will answer you and tell you great and mighty things you do not know. [Jeremiah 33:3 KJV]. From time immemorial, God has been inviting us to converse with Him about anything and everything. Inviting us to test Him with hard questions as the Queen of Sheba did when she visited King Solomon [1 Kings 10:1] as if there is anything that we can ask that God cannot answer. This was the invitation that He extended to the children of Israel, and with smoke, fire, thunder and earthquake, God came to His chosen people and with His own finger inscribed on tablets of stone His eternal words of instruction. I just taught my Children's Church group from Exodus chapter 20 on Sunday and marveled again at the wisdom and simplicity of God's commands given thousands of years ago yet still profoundly relevant today.

Sadly people tend to view the Ten Commandments from either one of two extremes: as suggestions, muttering darkly: 'Surely God you don't expect us to follow this punitive list of rules' OR as ten demands, groaning: 'God is the onerous task master who robs us of every delight'. Neither view is correct if we truly know and understand the heart of God [Exodus 34:6,7]. None of us can certainly attest to a character like that: immeasurably compassionate, gracious, forgiving, loving, and patient. That is the nature of the God who loves us and gave His Son that we may live forever with Him.

What does He tell us to do? The first four commandments instruct us in our relationship with Him, and He begins as it were at the beginning: *"You must not have any other god but me."* [Exodus 20: 3] Let's think about that one. No other gods. The definition itself refers to those deemed to have some measure of power over our lives. Service to these deities generally comes with a hefty price and only a modicum of temporary reward. The Egyptians had a plethora of gods who were believed to have authority over things like crops, health, weather, or their enemies. As God released each of the ten plagues, the gods of Egypt fell, revealing to the Egyptians' amazement that their gods were worthless, powerless to aid them against the might of I AM.

The same may be said for the gods that people have surrendered to in current society. Wealth, power, relationships, beauty, even cell phones and social media are worshipped by people to the point that they sell their souls for the opportunity to obtain some tangible measure of reward. The amount of time, resources and effort that people put into each one of these things indicates how important they've become to their happiness and contentment. Knowing our natures, that's why the Lord dictated the first commandment. We can't give Jesus a moment of our time or attention, if we've become seduced by these worldly things.

The second commandment builds on the first: *"you must not make for yourself an idol of any kind"* [Exodus 20:4]. Even before the incident with the golden calf, our heavenly Father understood people's desire for a tangible representation of God. What we see or touch, we deem as real in opposition to the faith that it takes to believe in a God that we cannot see. That's why this commandment warns against the trap of seeing to believe instead of believing without seeing. That's why we are instructed to *walk by faith and not by sight* [2 Corinthians 5:7 KJV]. It is by faith that we please God [Hebrews 11:6], and blessed are we if we do so, Jesus told His disciples [John 20:29]

This begs the question: have we set up any idols? We might not think of them in that way but consider for a moment - is there something that we can't imagine living without. Something that's so precious to us that if we didn't have it nothing else would matter. That, my friend, is an idol, and God asks that we set that aside for Him. He has to be first in our lives, before anything or anyone else. For we can't take those things to Heaven with us and if they won't make it there, of what value are they here? Paul makes it clear in his letter to the Corinthians whose cities were infested with idols [1 Corinthians 3:12-15].

The third commandment warns us not to *"misuse the name of the Lord your God"* [Exodus 20:7]. We're commanded not to speak His name in blasphemy, insincerity or as a curse. This is true for all people, but especially for believers as the Holy Spirit living within us will not allow us to speak those words [1 John 2:20-23]. Should we use His name in such a profane manner, then we truly need to re-examine our commitment to the Lord, ask for forgiveness and return to our first love.

The next, insincerity, suggests that we are not genuine in our love of God and casually sling His name around to appear pious or religious. A person who genuinely loves Jesus will treat His name with respect and reverence, addressing Him or talking to others about Him, with the recognition that we are using the name of the Holiest of the Holy Ones. The final way of using His name that this commandment warns against is in false attribution. What do I mean by that? It refers to those who attribute something to God that He has not said or done, suggesting that He has revealed something to us that He hasn't revealed to others. Such pride brings attention to us and not God which dishonors His name.

The fourth commandment: *Remember to observe the Sabbath day by keeping it holy"* [Exodus 20:8] struck me with great force recently. I'd always considered church an important part of my week, essential actually and anticipated going every Sunday. Yet I've discovered many who do not share my enthusiasm and consider church as a "maybe" rather than a "without a doubt." For some, church becomes a social event, a place to see friends, an obligation or a reluctant spiritual requirement. God wants us to rejoice at this opportunity to worship in His house [Psalm 122:1]. He knows attending church has the potential to reform our priorities, re-establish our purpose, and re-invigorate our labors. How can we desire Heaven, where every day is a Sabbath, a holy day to the Lord, if we don't desire church here, and we duck and dive to find an excuse not to go? Beloved, I can't stress enough how important this commandment is. Church may not be a perfect representation of our heavenly home, but it's God's invention and God's intention that we make the day we worship as one that honors His Name.

The first four commandments are summed up in Deuteronomy 6:5 and repeated by Jesus to the Pharisees as the first and greatest commandment in Matthew 22: 37: *"Love the Lord your God with all your heart, all your soul and all your mind."* That means with our entire being, nothing held back. Then He proceeds to say that the second is like it: *"Love your neighbor as yourself."* [Matthew 22:39; Romans 13:9] In loving others, the Apostle John advises we are showing our love for God [1 John 4:7,8].

What does this love for others look like? Commandment five explains: *"Honor your father and your mother. Then you will live a long, full life in the land the Lord your God is giving you."* [Exodus 20:12] Paul reminds us that this is the first commandment with a promise – long life [Ephesians 6:2,3]. With this instruction, God is saying that love for others must begin within the family. It must begin with children respecting their parents. When we value and appreciate them, we align ourselves with God's Word and God's will.

Of course, the first concern people mention is 'But God my parents don't do anything for which I can give them honor. They lie, steal, cheat, drink, beat me. How do I give such awful people respect? They have done nothing to deserve it.' Sadly, in too many cases, that may be true. How then do we align our obedience to God's Word with the cruel reality we know? Let's consider for a minute that God knows the inadequacy of our parents and every one of their sins. Even when He wrote this commandment, He knew our parents would fail us in so many ways. God doesn't qualify here that it's only perfect parents that are to be honored, or godly parents, or even good parents. He simply says, 'honor them'. This means that we are to recognize the role that God has given to them on our behalf. It signifies that their DNA made us, created us into the people that we are today. Perhaps their behavior can't be admired, and should they ask us to do something illegal or immoral then we must revert to the first four commandments that require us to put God first. Trust me, every parent will make mistakes and some far worse than others. Still we can honor their God-ordained place in our lives, even if we can't or shouldn't follow their practices or imitate their behavior.

Let me give you an example. My mother was totally opposed to me going into missions. She felt it was unnecessary and dangerous. I honored her request but prayed daily that if God wanted me to serve Him overseas, He would soften my mom's heart and she'd release me to go. God did just that and for almost half of my life that's what I've done. But I was able to put God first and honor my mother at the same time as desiring to serve God. I don't know how this may work out in your life, I only ask that you try honoring your parents and see what God will do - in you, and in them.

"You must not murder" is the sixth commandment [Exodus 20:13] That one seems quite obvious for we've developed laws that forbid such behavior as well, but Jesus takes it even further, commanding us to not even call people fools [Mathew 5:21-22]. Love doesn't just restrain us from inflicting bodily harm, but it constrains us from speaking in an ugly manner to others for Jesus knows that out of our mouth our heart speaks [Matthew 15:18].

The seventh commandment *"You must not commit adultery"* [Exodus 20:14] instructs us to keep our marriage bed holy [Hebrews 13:4], honor our vows to our spouse and before God, and maintain a protective barrier around our family. Commandment eight demands that we *"not steal"* [Exodus 20:15]. All of us recognize the violation that we feel when someone has taken something of ours without permission. Stealing is an act of selfishness, indicating that our own desires far exceed our respect for the belongings of others. Nothing breaks a relationship faster than when someone takes what we've not offered. Commandment nine warns us to *"not testify falsely against your neighbor"* [Exodus 20:16]. In today's language that means we're not to lie. This is another trust-breaker. If we can't believe someone to tell us the truth than we can't trust them for anything – certainly not our friendship, and when a lie is spoken, love is broken.

Finally, commandment ten instructs us not to desire our neighbor's house, wife, servants, animals or other goods [Exodus 20:17] In today's language the word "covet" means that we're jealous of or crave to have what belongs to another. Although this may be the last commandment and may appear to be the least offensive, in fact, if broken it really cascades into all the other commandments, for envy may lead to lying, which may lead to stealing, which may lead to desiring someone else's spouse, which may lead to murder. Thus, it's by no means innocuous, but equally as deadly as all the others, for when thoughts become words, and words become actions then relationships are destroyed.

Thus, the question is: how do we live by the Ten Commandments? How do we consolidate them into two: loving God and loving others? The reality is that we can't do this on our own. Living the Christian life is not for weaklings. It takes a courageous individual, surrendered to the will of God and empowered by the Holy Spirit [Colossians 1:29]. Fortunately, our God is willing to pour out His grace into our lives to make this possible.

The Miracle of God's Grace

Moses watched as God wrote with His finger on stone tablets, forming the Ten Commandment. Over the next few days, Moses listened as God instructed him in the fair treatment of slaves [Exodus 21], justice [Exodus 23], the tabernacle's design [Exodus 25 – 27, 30-31] and the priest's attire [Exodus 28,29]. While Moses was basking in God's glory, the people were shuffling about nervously, wondering when or if they'd see their leader again. Finally, they decided they'd waited long enough and stomped up to Aaron with yet another set of demands: *"Make us some gods who can lead us. We don't know what happened to this fellow Moses"*. [Exodus 32:1]

Did Aaron balk at their profane request? Did he warn them against acting so rashly? Did he come to Moses' rescue and say: 'Hang on another minute! After all God and my brother have done, can't you trust that he's coming back to lead us into the Promised Land.' Sadly, he didn't do any one of those things. He didn't defend either God's character or his brother's.

If you've ever found yourself betrayed by a friend or family member and wondered: 'How could they do this to me?' Aaron's behavior proves that anyone can collapse under pressure and when it's a million strong, the burden to give in is even greater. Does that make Aaron's choice acceptable? Absolutely not. But it does help to consider how vulnerable we are to cave in the face of stress and how essential it is that we wear the full armor of God to resist the devil and make him flee [Ephesians 6:10-18]. Aaron's weakness reminds us to get spiritually dressed every day so we're ready for whatever attack may come our way. Clearly, Aaron wasn't ready. When the rebellious crowd complained, he gave them what they asked for, even though he knew it was wrong.

What were his first instructions to this cantankerous mob? 'Give me your jewelry, the baubles the Egyptians gave you when you left Egypt' [Exodus 32:2]. Had the Lord intended for this plunder to go to the construction of idols? Of course not, but sadly this wealth was squandered on the enemy. We're informed that when Aaron took the gold, he melted it down, and molded it into the shape of a calf [Exodus 32: 4]. Why a calf? This shape represented the Egyptian god Apis, a powerful deity that was believed to mediate between humans and the divine, providing them with strength and fertility. It was a recognizable image for the Israelites worship and likely they believed such qualities would be necessary for the treacherous journey ahead.

Ever since they'd left Egypt the Israelites had expressed their desire to return to their captivity, longing for the food, safety and now even the worship of their oppressors' useless gods. And Aaron made it possible. Indeed, when the people saw the golden calf they enthusiastically declared: *"O Israel, these are the gods who brought you out of the land of Egypt!"* [Exodus 32:4] Hadn't they already seen how completely God routed every one of the Egyptian gods? Hadn't they realized the blood of the spotless lamb withstood the angel of death? How could they possibly turn their backs so quickly, relinquishing the one true God who'd rescued them?

As He finished his last instructions to Moses, God heard the people's unabashed merriment and His heart froze. He knew what they were doing and why they'd rejected Him. He couldn't bear it. He turned to Moses: *"Your people whom you brought from the land of Egypt have corrupted themselves."* [Exodus 32:7]. He was ready to destroy this rebellious rabble and lead Moses into the Promised Land alone [Exodus 32:10]. Amazingly, despite all Moses had endured, still he interceded for them. He stood in the gap, protecting both God's character and these thankless people. He begged: *"**Turn away from**"* *your fierce anger.* **Change your mind** *about this terrible disaster you have threatened against your people!* **Remember** *your servants Abraham, Isaac, and Jacob.*" [Exodus 32:12,13]

Moses reminded God of the people He'd miraculously rescued. Not only that but he didn't want God to be reviled by the Egyptians as a merciless God. He prompted God to remember His ancient covenant to Abraham in which He'd promised descendants and land. He recapped God's faithful character and changeless nature, prophesying the New Testament hymn which declared: *"If we are unfaithful, he remains faithful, for he cannot deny who he is."* [2 Timothy 2:13] With these words Moses convinced God to change His mind and show mercy instead of issuing the well-deserved judgement.

Yet as Moses headed down the mountain and heard the revelry, he was so overwhelmed at the carnality before him that his anger burned. In his rage, *"[h]e threw the stone tablets to the ground, smashing them at the foot of the mountain. He took the calf they had made and burned it. Then he ground it into powder, threw it into the water, and forced the people to drink it."* [Exodus 32:19,20] Do you think as the people chewed the gravel, they realized what they'd done? Or would they just gulp it down because they were used to dirt in their mouths. We are only left to wonder.

Then Moses turned to Aaron whose paltry excuse shocks even us. He meekly deferred to Moses as his leader and then accused others, saying 'these evil people made me do it.' He seems to insinuate that he just threw in the jewelry and out popped the calf. Really? Now there were lots of miracles that have been recorded, but this just isn't one of them. The reality is that Aaron had stood before the fires and watched as the gold turned to liquid, then waited for it to cool before taking a special tool and carefully fashioning the molten gold into the shape of a calf. He was part of the process from beginning to end. This just didn't happen; he did it. Probably with disgust, Moses turned from his brother to the people: *"All of you who are on the LORD's side, come here and join me"* [Exodus 32:26] and the Levites stepped forward, establishing themselves from that moment as God's people.

Once again Moses intercedes for the people offering to have his own name erased from God's record book [Exodus 32:32]. He was willing to lose everything, even eternity for the people he was called to lead. Can we say the same? Can we offer such devoted intercession? Yet there would remain consequences for their blasphemy [Exodus 32:35], just as Jesus warned that there would be [Matthew 12:36]. This should sober us not to play games with the Lord and dance with the devil. As Joshua would years later advise the Israelites, we have to choose who we'll serve [Joshua 24:15]. We have to be careful where we give our hearts. Foolish choices could cost our lives, even our eternity.

A Miraculous Messenger

We left the Israelites with the gravel of their graven image scratching their throats and the Levites separating the faithful from the rebellious. The stone tablets carrying the sacred Ten Commandments were shattered on the mountainside and new tablets were constructed not by the finger of God, but by the calloused hand of Moses. But the words were the same – ten instructions to restore the covenant promises of love and loyalty between God and His People.

The journey through the wilderness was treacherous and the Israelites' faith was shaky at best. God, we read in the book of Leviticus, provided stringent instructions on worship, relationships, even their health and welfare. The tribe of Levi, from which Moses and Aaron hailed, were assigned to the priesthood and required to offer sacrifices to restore the people back to God. Yet even though God gave them careful instructions on how to complete their offerings, Aaron's sons Nadab and Abihu acted rashly, offending God with unholy fire and losing their lives for their disrespect [Leviticus 10]. Even Aaron and Miriam challenged God, questioning His choice of Moses as leader, but Moses' holiness and humility confirmed his position and Miriam suffered leprosy for her insolence. Moses, ever the faithful and forgiving intermediary, interceded for her and God showed mercy once again [Numbers 12].

Finally, they were on the cusp of Canaan, the Promised Land,

and Moses selected twelve strong men, one from each tribe to spy out the land. They were overwhelmed with what they discovered: clusters of grapes so heavy it took two men to carry them, fertile soil so rich that seeds leapt from the earth to sprout into luscious crops. The spies reported their observations: a bountiful land defended by undefeatable giants [Numbers 13]. Only Joshua and Caleb believed God was greater than their enemies. Sadly, the grumblers were louder, and the people refused to listen to the wise counsel of Moses and Aaron [Numbers 14]. Once again Moses had to intercede for the people and God relented, but there was a fatal cost. They were not allowed to enter the Promised Land. Only Caleb and Joshua would set their feet on the promised soil and eats its fruits. When the people heard this, they were grieved, admitted their sin, and thought they could recover from delayed obedience. They thought that with a word of contrition they could receive the blessings, but Moses knew otherwise. They may have gained a reprieve, but their sin cost them the Promised Land; they may have gained their lives but lost the blessing.

What recklessness to think that we can say 'I'm sorry' and that's enough to receive all that God has offered? This is often seen by business people who think that they can do evil against their employees or cheat their customers or defy government policy and won't suffer the consequences of their crimes. Or pastors who think they can sin against God and others and then continue in ministry as if there is no consequence for their wrongdoing.

God does forgive if a person's heart is genuinely repentant, but it doesn't mean that there isn't consequences. We have to be willing to bear the penalty, no matter how painful it may be, for even in those moments, God is at work in our character to forge us into the person He intends us to be. We can't rush His processes of redemption, by relying on easy grace. Jesus had to pay a terrible price for our sins, and it wasn't enough for Him to petition in the Garden of Gethsemane with drops of blood pouring out of His skin; He had to bear the soldier's whip for our healing and the cross for our salvation [1 Peter 2:24].

Still God miraculously led the children of Israel, aiding them in defeating the Amorite king Sihon and Bashon king Og. Israel's battle successes struck fear in the hearts of the Moabites, who sought spiritual help, requesting an internationally reputed diviner Balaam to petition for divine intervention. Balaam, a dabbler in celestial forces, willingly received his instruction from any deity who would speak to him; thus, when the Lord Himself speaks to him about King Balak's request, he has no problem responding [Numbers 22]. Yet God knows Balaam's greedy and fickle heart and sends an angel to obstruct his path. Unaware of the warrior angel blocking the road, Balaam beats his frightened donkey who finally collapses in fear.

It was then that the Lord opened the donkey's mouth to rebuke his faithless, cruel master: *"What have I done to you that deserves your beating me three times?"* [Numbers 22:28] Balaam, in his rage, didn't even realize that his donkey had been given the power of human speech and shouted at him: *"'You have made me look like a fool! If I had a sword with me, I would kill you!'"* [Numbers 22:29] The small, humble donkey persisted: *"But I am the same donkey you have ridden all your life. Have I ever done anything like this before?"* [Numbers 22:30] It was only then that God revealed the sword-wielding angel to Balaam. At last Balaam got it. He was in the presence of a heavenly messenger and it was only by his donkey's bravery that he wasn't struck down [Numbers 22:32-34]. Balaam even promised to speak only the words that God put in his mouth and proceeded to deliver five prophecies which blessed Israel and cursed their enemies [Numbers 23,24].

Sadly, however, Balaam didn't learn from his furry friend. His heart remained prideful and idolatrous. Although he didn't openly curse Israel, he enticed them to worship Baal, the false god of the Moabites [Numbers 25]. What did he gain for his efforts? Wealth and power – but only briefly. Ultimately, the cost for his treachery was death. He was killed by the Israelites, probably while still practicing his divination [Joshua 13:22]. The apostle Peter used him as a warning against those who seek to seduce a believer into false worship [2 Peter 2].

What does Balaam's story teach us? God may use the most unlikely messengers to prevent us from going the wrong way, and to realize the folly of our attitude or behavior. As Peter warned his congregations, we also want to stay clear of false teachers, who despite their good standing may try to lead us astray. How gracious God is that He always makes a way of escape.

The Miracle of Discipline

We can't read the story of Balaam and his eloquent donkey without getting a smile on our face. Although it's a serious lesson, nonetheless it's the humorous and unassuming messenger that tickles us. God wanted to bless His people and, regardless of their enemy's efforts, He made sure it happened, even if His human courier was less than perfect. In the same way, God wants to ensure that a blessing is pronounced over our lives even if others are resistant.

However, there are times He must also deliver consequences should our pride or disobedience warrant it. Even Moses learned that fateful lesson. For decades he'd served the Lord, sacrificing his comfort and safety to lead a grumbling, rebellious band through the wilderness; interceding for their deliverance; even offering his own place in eternity to ensure that God would forgive their blatant sin.

Despite his years of faithfulness, there was one moment when his actions cost him the Promised Land: the waters of Meribah. The thirsty Israelites were once again whining about the lack of water. When they finally reached a stream, they discovered the waters were bitter and, with their usual impatience, turned violent against their leader. In desperation, Moses sought the Lord for His help. God answered him and specifically instructed him what to do: take the staff, assembly the people, speak to the rock [Numbers 20:6-8]. The instructions were simple and clear. I'm not sure what happened between Moses humbly listening to the Lord and standing before the people, staff in his hand, but something did, and it wasn't good. Here's what Moses said: *"Listen, you rebels!" he shouted. "Must we bring you water from this rock?" Then Moses raised his hand and struck the rock twice with the staff, and water gushed out"*. [Numbers 20:10-11]

Perhaps Moses looked at all those angry faces. Perhaps he even saw the rocks in their hands ready to stone him and he'd simply had enough. After all, hadn't God just spoken to him? Hadn't God, the Creator of the Universe just given him the power to produce water from the rock? Why should he have to put up with the constant complaints of this rabble? Thus, he shouted at them: *"Must we bring you water from this rock."* Then he slammed the rock twice. But that's not what God said. *"Speak to the rock"*. Those were His words.

Surely, it's no big deal. It's just words after all. And we all get angry and speak out in haste. We all get tired of the demands on us. We all feel like pounding something occasionally. But it was a big deal to God and His reaction to what Moses did is a sobering reminder to all of us. Moses had been given a heavenly calling, hailed from a burning bush and commanded to "set the captives free". Selected from all the people on the earth to hear directly from God with fire and power. He was equipped to display God's might through fantastic plagues, the parting of the Sea, the crushing of the enemy, the daily provision of food; all amazing miracles of what God can do. But Moses turned their attention from God to him.

God knew what Moses' actions signified: *"Because you did not trust me enough to demonstrate my holiness to the people of Israel, you will not lead them into the land I am giving them!"* [Numbers 20:12] God called his and Aaron's actions a betrayal: *"For both of you betrayed me with the Israelites at the waters of Meribah at Kadesh in the wilderness of Zin. You failed to demonstrate my holiness to the people of Israel there"*. [Deuteronomy 32:51]

Time after time when Pharaoh threatened or the people rebelled, God protected Moses, declaring emphatically that Moses was His chosen leader. Besides showing him His glory, God hand-delivered His own personally crafted instructions. Twice God offered to make Moses a great nation when the people would have mumbled and grumbled their way to oblivion. God had given Moses great personal attention and power. Because He trusted him with so much, a great deal was required of him. Jesus explains the connection: *"A servant who knows what the master wants, but isn't prepared and doesn't carry out those instructions, will be severely punished. But someone who does not know, and then does something wrong, will be punished only lightly. When someone has been given much, much will be required in return; and when someone has been entrusted with much, even more will be required"*. [Luke 12:47,48]

Through thunder, lightning and smoke God appeared and His glorious light was so blinding that Moses had to cover his face for the residual glory of this divine encounter [Exodus 34:33-35]. Have any of us had that heavenly glow after speaking with the Lord? We may feel like it and others may see a change in us, but I don't know of anyone shining so brightly that a veil was needed to diminish their brilliance. Not only did the brilliance of the Lord rub off on Moses, but they also conversed as friends [Exodus 33:11]. What a wonder to be called a friend of God.

Moses knew God looked upon him with favor and felt so comfortable and confident in his relationship with the Lord that he held this conversation with Him: *"If it is true that you look favorably on me, let me know your ways so I may understand you more fully and continue to enjoy your favor."* [Exodus 33:13] God reassured him: *"I will personally go with you, Moses, and I will give you rest—everything will be fine for you."* [Exodus 33:14]

These words made Moses so bold that he asked to see the Lord, and God did so, tucking Moses into a crevice so His goodness wouldn't consume him [Exodus 33:19-23]. Haven't many of us read Exodus 33 and said 'God I wish that were me. I wish I could see your glory'. Yet Moses had witnessed such wonders from the opening of the Red Sea to the daily provision of manna and quail. Witnessing such astounding events and enjoying such an intimate relationship required a deeper level of submission and obedience, a humble acknowledgement of His holiness. Their close relationship, friend to favored friend demanded a high level of respect. Thus, Moses' careless actions grieved the heart of God. Did God fulfill the miracle of bringing water from the rock? Yes! But oh, the cost of the miracle. Even though Moses begged for an opportunity to enter the Promised Land, God was firm.

What do we learn from this? We must be careful how we treat the Lord. He isn't our buddy although we may be friends. We can't be casual about what He says as if it's an acquaintance on Facebook or Twitter. God is holy and so is His Word. If we teach or lead, we need to acknowledge who He is and act accordingly. His miracles are His works – not ours. We can't let anger control our tongues or our actions. James warns teachers that they will be judged more strictly [James 3:1], and spiritual leaders are held to account [Hebrews 13:17].

So, what must we do? It begins by treating Him, His Word and His instructions with reverent respect. Paul tells Timothy: *"Keep a close watch on how you live and on your teaching. Stay true to what is right for the sake of your own salvation and the salvation of those who hear you."* [1 Timothy 4:16]. Then we can know *"with confidence and a clear conscience that we have lived with a God-given holiness and sincerity in all our dealings. We have depended on God's grace, not on our own human wisdom. That is how we have conducted ourselves before the world"* [2 Corinthians 1:12].

God's discipline is a miracle of His grace. He corrects us as a father does his son [Hebrews 12:6-11]. The next time He does so, be grateful. He is confirming His love while sharing His holiness.

Miraculous Appointments

Slowly, step by final step, Moses climbed to the top of Mount Nebo and stood on Pisgah Peak. From this vantage point, Moses could see the entire land of Canaan spread out before him. The land of milk and honey. The land God had promised his people for centuries; the land Moses longed to enter but could not and he understood why. His rash action of betrayal denied him that opportunity.

It's disappointing not to reach the goal that's been our life's work. No wonder Paul says that he doesn't want to run the race and not receive the prize [1Corinthians 9:24; Philippians 2:16; Hebrews 12:1]. The Christian life is indeed a race and we want to run it to victory, serving Him faithfully, worshipping Him sincerely, and honoring Him reverently. That is what He calls us to do so that we can receive the prize that He's promised, the crown of life. Yet even if Moses didn't enter the Promised Land, he was still blessed. He was still vigorously healthy when God gathered him to Himself [Deuteronomy 34:7], and even though he didn't gain entrance into the land of milk and honey, he still stood with Jesus on the Mount of Transfiguration [Luke 9:28-36] and has eternity with Christ. That is the ultimate prize that we all want to achieve.

And God's plan was still unfolding. For those four decades, a young man walked by Moses' side, learned from his example and experience. He walked the mountain top and the valley, and from these life lessons and Moses' gentle laying on of hands he was anointed to lead [Deuteronomy 34: 9]. Now was his time to lead, and God would not fail him. God's assurance was firm and absolute. All the promises He'd given Moses were now transferred to Joshua. None would stand against him. The land was his. What a powerful word of blessing. [Joshua 1:1-9].

Yet still Joshua's knees trembled, and his hands shook. This was a huge undertaking and he'd been there to witness Moses' struggles. Could he do it, he wondered? God reassured him: "*Be strong and courageous*" [Joshua 1:6]. Four times in this chapter God tells Joshua to be strong and courageous. He knows that Joshua feels overwhelmed by the responsibility of leadership. Even though he'd walked beside Moses his mentor, watched what he did, how he did it and supported him in it, he was afraid. His spiritual father was gone. All that he'd worked for was now his responsibility. What a breathless place to be. Undoubtedly, he was trembling. If not on the outside, then certainly on the inside.

Not only that, but he was facing another water obstacle – the River of Jordan was raging at flood level. What would God have him do? "*Be careful to obey all the instructions Moses gave you. Do not deviate from them, turning either to the right or to the left. Then you will be successful in everything you do. Study this Book of Instruction continually. Meditate on it day and night so you will be sure to obey everything written in it. Only then will you prosper and succeed in all you do.*" [Joshua 1:7,8] Here's the ticket to success: Obey the instructions we've been given. Don't get muddled by hindrances. Do what His Word says.

Following the earlier wisdom of Moses, Joshua sent out two spies to look over the land. The fortified city of Jericho, their first point of contact on the other side of the Jordan, was strategically located on a significant trade route. Securing this city was key to them entering the Promised Land. It is here we meet Rahab.

The spies knew the magnitude of their assignment and were calculated in their tactics. Although a prostitute may seem like an unlikely ally, the spies were quite shrewd; they sought out a woman already known to welcome strange men into her home. Even when their visit was discovered, she risked her own life to protect them, taking them to her roof and covering them with sheaves of grain. Then when the soldiers beat on her door, she concocted a believable story [Joshua 2:4,5] What a clever woman. After safely secreting the spies onto her roof, she sent the soldiers on a wild goose chase outside the city.

Why did she risk her life and her city? She knew Almighty God, knew what He'd already done for the Children of Israel and what He was about to do [Joshua 2:9-11]. She had unshakeable faith. Although she hadn't walked through the Red Sea, eaten the manna or quail, drank the fresh waters from the rock, yet she believed in the power and mystery of God. God was going to give them her land and her city. For her, it was that simple. She only had one request – save my family. This statement beyond all others revealed the loving heart of Rahab.

Let's consider who she was and what she did for a living. She engaged in prostitution. That's not a career choice that endears someone to their family. It was likely her family rejected her, yet she didn't hold it against them. When danger was coming, she wanted them safe. Perhaps some of us have also had family members who've abandoned us. We've felt the pain of their rejection. Are we willing to speak to God on behalf of their salvation? Are we asking God to help them through life's battles? Rahab showed us how.

What about the spies? They were impressed with her faith; encouraged by her convictions; grateful for her protection. Thus, they agreed to her request, promising that if she displayed a scarlet rope and gathered all her family under her roof, all of them would be safe. A scarlet rope. How similar to the scarlet rope God suspends to deliver us – the blood of Jesus Christ His Son which cleanses us from all unrighteousness and delivers us from sin and death [1 Peter 1:2; 1 John 1:7; Revelation 1:5].

Before we meet Rahab and her scarlet cord again, another miracle occurred for the children of Israel. In order to enter the Promised Land, the huge group of people had to cross the flooded Jordan River. God's strategy: Send ahead the priests with the Ark of the Covenant. Follow them. Purify yourselves. Miracles will happen [Joshua 3: 2-5]. And that is what they did. As soon as the priests reached the water's edge, the river stopped flowing and the waters built up, allowing all the people to walk across on dry ground.

Another miraculous crossing, different from the Red Sea, but no less extraordinary. But this one must be remembered. Joshua instructed twelve men to gather twelve stones from the dry river bed and create a celebratory memorial. When future generations asked about these stones, they were to tell of God's supernatural intervention.

What miracle has God done to help you receive the promises that He's given you? Have you collected memorials to help you remember them? Just as Joshua wanted the Children of Israel to remember their miraculous crossing, so God wants us to remember the remarkable ways He's delivered us.

The journey recorded in Joshua 1-3 is a remarkable story of God speaking into people's lives. He told Joshua to be courageous; He told Rahab to believe; He told the Israelites to remember. Then He gave them miraculous signs: the divided Jordan River; the suspended scarlet cord; the constructed memorial. Each one illustrates the miraculous work of God to save and redeem. How can we apply this to our lives today?

Miraculous Signs

For as long as Joshua was leading them, the Israelites followed the Lord [Joshua 24:31], but once he passed away, they did whatever made them happy [Judges 17:6]. The consequences, as God warned, were catastrophic, and in their anguish, they cried to the Lord for help. This is where we meet up with Gideon in Judges chapter 6, a hero sent to rescue them from their self-inflicted difficulties.

It's tragic how hardships so often lead us back to God. But we must remember, that isn't the way God wants us to have a relationship with Him – with us heading the wrong way, dabbling in darkness and God leading us back to His light through various adversities [Colossians 1:13]. He'd so much rather we stayed on the right path and lived in His blessings.

It seems the Israelites were still learning this lesson. Their land of milk and honey had definitely soured. The Midianites, the neighbors they couldn't seem to get rid of were harassing them, destroying their crops and stealing their livestock. Life was miserable. Desperately they cried for help, and God sent them a messenger who reminded them of God's deliverance and their faithlessness [Judges 6:7-10]. Even though they'd stopped listening to Him, He still heard their cries and, as the book of Judges illustrates, sent them a rescuer. This time it was Gideon, a man who certainly wasn't expecting the call: *"Mighty hero, the* LORD *is with you!"* [Judges 6:12] Gideon seemed unimpressed with the inspirational greeting, concentrating instead on the problems instead of the promises. *"Sir,"* Gideon *replied, "if the* LORD *is with us, why has all this happened to us? And where are all the miracles our ancestors told us about? Didn't they say, 'The* LORD *brought us up out of Egypt'? But now the* LORD *has abandoned us and handed us over to the Midianites."* [Judges 6:13]

Cheeky fellow, isn't he? Gideon blamed God for all their problems. 'Why is this happening? Where are the miracles? The Lord left us and gave us to our enemies.' A little whiny, isn't it? Not much repentance or even recognition of responsibility. Yet God stayed on task and kept Gideon focused*: "Go with the strength you have, and rescue Israel from the Midianites. I am sending you!"* [Judges 6:14]. God knew He'd already equipped Gideon with the abilities he'd need to complete the mission.

Yet Gideon wasn't convinced, reciting his insignificant family and personal weaknesses. He believed his family tree determined his ability to serve God. He seemed to be saying that 'since I come from a poor, inconsequential family, that makes me nothing, too'. Does that sound like us sometimes? We believe that who our family is determines who we'll be. We limit ourselves by what we think about our family, when in fact the only family connection that's important is the one we have with Jesus Christ [Ephesians 1:18].

God said that to Gideon. He was for him and that alone made him victorious [Romans 8:31]. God doesn't doubt it. And neither should we when He calls us. But Gideon wasn't yet convinced and asked the angel to wait while he brought a sacrifice. You can almost hear the angel chuckle at Gideon's doubt but nonetheless he waited. When Gideon returned with the offering, the angel ignited it with one touch and then vanished. That got Gideon's attention as did the Spirit's next instruction: 'Clean up this place. It's a mess.' He asked him to tear down all his father's altars to Baal. He needed Gideon to separate himself from his family's faithlessness and establish his own commitment. Like Joshua, he needed to determine who he'd serve. It was a brave, bold act, but Gideon, by the cover of night completed the task. By morning the village discovered the desecration of their idol. They were furious and demanded Gideon's execution. Surprisingly, his father came to his defense, demanding that Baal should protect his own altar.

God protected his warrior, Gideon, in the same manner He protected His own Son when mobs tried to stone Him before His time of ultimate sacrifice. Others such as Esther, Daniel, Shadrach, Meshach and Abednego also stand as living examples of God's divine protection. With each one, God clothed them with power to accomplish His purpose as He did with Gideon [Judges 6:34]. Yet despite all of this, at this moment of reckoning, Gideon began to tremble. Was God really calling him? 'Prove it', he told God, and outlined his specific plan [Judges 6:36-40].

Gideon was overwhelmed. He needed to be reassured that God was calling him to this great task. He needed to see a miracle to believe God would do the impossible. God didn't flinch – wet fleece/dry fleece – it was all the same to Him. At last, Gideon was secure and said in effect 'Ok, God. I'm ready. Let's do this.' But God wasn't finished with Gideon yet. Before they went into battle, God told him he had too many soldiers, 22,000 to be exact, who lacked the courage to fight.

Even with this culling, there were still too many; too many to boast of their skills as a warrior when the battle was won rather than the ingenuity of God. Thus, God tested them when they bent down by the river to drink. The warriors who cupped water in their hands and lapped it up with their tongues were selected. This left only 300 men. Have you ever wondered why God tested them in this manner? Likely He needed to see which men were vigilant, always watching for danger. Those who bent with their face into the water could not see if an enemy approached and were not ready to defend themselves or their fellow warriors; those who lapped the water from their hands could observe what or who was around them and leap into battle mode in an instant. These were the warriors God needed [Judges 7]

Yet Gideon, already fearful and now with only 300 men against a massive army, was terrified. How could they ever win, he wondered? God wanted to encourage him and on the night before the battle, He sent him into the Midianite camp. There he found a restless soldier recounting a frightening dream foretelling an Israelite victory. Upon hearing these words, from the enemy no less, Gideon was at last convinced.

A sword, a ram's horn, a hidden torch and a pottery jar. That's all it took. With just 300 men guided by God's unique battle strategy, victory was achieved. Stationed around the perimeter of the Midianite camp, this small army erupted with sound and light: a blast from the horn, a smashing of the jar, a burst of light, a blast from the horn, and a shout. In the ensuing chaos, the Midianites panicked and began to destroy one another. With a band of brave soldiers in the hands of the Lord, the massive Midianite army was annihilated.

Once again God does the impossible. We may doubt Him; we may need to see sign after sign of His presence, His power and His purpose, but still God prevails. The story of Gideon is a lesson to inspire us when we face overwhelming odds. Nothing is too great for God: no army or difficulty. When He's with us, He fortifies us, and our success is assured. Trust Him for it today.

Miraculous Redemption

Sometimes when life knocks us about, we can't seem to find the strength to pick ourselves back up. Naomi must have felt that way. First a famine in Bethlehem compelled her husband to move his wife and sons to the foreign country of Moab. Once there they dedicated themselves to settling in and making a go of it. Before their sons were old enough to marry, Naomi's husband Elimelech died, leaving Naomi a widow with sons still to raise. In time, the boys married Moabite women, but a decade later, her sons also died. Now Naomi was alone with only her daughters-in-law, Orpah and Ruth, to support her. The land of the Moabites had brought her nothing but grief, so Naomi drew the young widows to her and told them her plan: 'The drought is over in Judah and people are now prospering. I'm going to return to Bethlehem to my people and I encourage you to return home to your families. You are both young and can remarry. I have nothing more to offer and will not force you to come with me. Go home, dear ones; it's time'.

The young women grieved. They didn't want to leave Naomi. She'd been kind to them and cared for them even though they came from different customs and religious traditions. Both young women resisted. 'We want to stay with you', they said, but Naomi was insistent and finally Orpah gathered her things and with a sad wave slowly made her way back to her family. With Ruth it was different. Her jaw was set, her attitude, while humble, was determined. 'I'm staying with you', she said resolutely, and made a vow: *"Wherever you go, I will go; wherever you live, I will live. Your people will be my people, and your God will be my God. Wherever you die, I will die, and there I will be buried. May the LORD punish me severely if I allow anything but death to separate us!"* [Ruth 1:16,17]

Here was an opportunity for Ruth to remain with her own people and worship the god Chemosh as she'd been raised. She could live within her own cultural customs and resume her life as a Moabite, but she refused. She'd lived for over decade with this Jewish family and she'd not just adopted but embraced their practices and spiritual convictions. She refused to turn back now.

What could one say against such commitment? Naomi relented, knowing it was a difficult journey and she was an old woman; she was grateful for the gentle companionship and support of Ruth, and so they set out. Although it was only a thirty-mile trip, it required them to climb over 2,000 feet in elevation to reach the village of Bethlehem. Quite exhausting for such an elderly, grieving woman. When they finally arrived and were greeted by Naomi's surprised, but welcoming family, she was shame-faced with sorrow, offering Mara as her name to denote her bitterness. She'd left her home a young wife and mother of two strapping sons but returned widowed and childless with only a foreign daughter-in-law at her side. Her desolation was a painful reminder of what she'd lost. She didn't yet recognize what she'd gained.

To stave off starvation, Ruth offered to work in the field as a gleaner, an age-old Jewish custom which allowed the poor to collect the left-over sheaves of grain. It was a dangerous job for a woman, especially a hated Moabite, as she was vulnerable to mockery and even assault by those laboring in the field, but her industry was recognized and respected by the foreman who commended her to the field's owner. She had 'coincidentally' entered the field of a close relative, an honorable man who rewarded her service by providing not only his protection but provision as well, saying: *"May the Lord, the God of Israel, under whose wings you have come to take refuge, reward you fully for what you have done."* [Ruth 2:12]

One harvest season slipped into another, and Ruth persevered in the heat of the harvest sun, working faithfully in Boaz's fields throughout the seasons. Her diligence won the approval of the workers, gleaners and even Boaz himself who noted her self-less dedication to Naomi. His thoughtful generosity touched Naomi and got her to thinking, 'perhaps God was doing something here, something unexpected but wonderful'. She presented her plan to Ruth: 'Prepare yourself, present yourself and pray' [Ruth 3:3,4]. Good advice for any of us needing a new beginning.

Nonetheless, Naomi's instruction for Ruth to place herself at the feet of a sleeping Boaz sounds strange to our modern sensibilities although it represented an ancient Jewish tradition. Although frightened by the potential consequences, Ruth trusted her mother-in-law, and knew she had her best interests at heart. Thus dressed, perfumed and ready, Ruth set forth, placing herself in a position more frightening than her decision to leave her people and join Naomi's family and adhere to her faith traditions. In the dark of night, watching and waiting in the shadows, Ruth observed Boaz lie down and pull the blankets over him. Hearing his gentle snores, she crept forward and, carefully lifting the edge of the blanket, tucked herself in at Boaz's feet.

Can you imagine how she must have felt, breathless with a wild combination of fear and excitement, knowing that what took place in the next hours would determine her future? If Boaz rejected her, not only would she suffer horrible humiliation, but, in all likelihood, the protection and provision that she and Naomi had enjoyed throughout the harvests would disappear, leaving them defenseless and exposed. The distress of such a possibility must have chilled Ruth to the core, yet despite the terror, she remained still and quiet. Only her lips moved in silent petition as she clenched her hands in prayer.

Then she felt him stir and as he stretched his legs felt him startle as he bumped her shoulder. To his harsh question: *"Who are you?"* she responded as Naomi had scripted her: *"I am your servant Ruth. Spread the corner of your covering over me, for you are my family redeemer."* Boaz knew precisely what she meant by this request and to her immense relief saw his worried expression give way to a beaming smile: *"The* LORD *bless you, my daughter!"* Boaz exclaimed. *"You are showing even more family loyalty now than you did before, for you have not gone after a younger*

*man, whether rich or poor. Now don't worry about a thing, my daughter.
I will do what is necessary, for everyone in town knows you are a virtuous
woman."* [Ruth 3:9-11]

His answer revealed his delight in Ruth's choice. She selected him,
a more mature man, than someone younger. He then commended
her for her virtuous character, one known and recognized by those in
their village. Finally, he explained why he hadn't pursued her already.
According to Jewish tradition, another man had first rights, but he
promised to talk with him, and should this man decline the offer to be
her kinsmen redeemer, Boaz would gladly fulfill the role.

With the morning light, Boaz set out for the city gates, the place
where all legal transactions were witnessed. Upon seeing the relative
in question, Boaz presented his case, offering him the opportunity
to purchase Elimelech's land. Initially the man heartily agreed, but
when he learned that he must also take Ruth, the foreign daughter-
in-law as his wife, he hastily declined. Taking Ruth as a bride would
jeopardize his own inheritance and standing in the community as she
was a foreigner and he undoubtedly didn't wish to add such a woman
to his collection of wives. Likely he'd not familiarized himself with
Naomi's sorrowful return or Ruth's stellar character or he wouldn't have
originally leapt at the economic opportunity and then backpedaled so
quickly at the realization it required him to take a foreign wife.

Standing tall and face creased in a huge smile, Boaz declared to the
council of elders his decision: 'I will take the land and Ruth as my wife'.
His forceful assertion left not a shred of doubt as to his commitment to
Naomi and Ruth. He would redeem them at any cost, and the elders'
affirmation was immediate and emphatic. Moreover, they pronounced
an incredible blessing over Ruth, ensuring her adoption and acceptance
within the Jewish community: *"May the LORD make this woman who is
coming into your home like Rachel and Leah, from whom all the nation
of Israel descended! May you prosper in Ephrathah and be famous in
Bethlehem. And may the LORD give you descendants by this young woman
who will be like those of our ancestor Perez, the son of Tamar and Judah."*
[Ruth 4:11,12]

These respected men declared a supernatural blessing over Ruth and Boaz, pronouncing prosperity and progeny to their marriage. It was a wonderful community moment, establishing Boaz and Ruth's exciting spiritual and economic future. Clearly, they were loved and respected by all, a proclamation declared upon the birth of their first child: *"Praise the LORD, who has now provided a redeemer for your family! May this child be famous in Israel. May he restore your youth and care for you in your old age. For he is the son of your daughter-in-law who loves you and has been better to you than seven sons!"* [Ruth 4:14,15]

Indeed, Boaz and Ruth would be great-grandparents to the godly king David and ancestors in the line, generations later, of our Savior Jesus Christ [Matthew 1]. It's breathtaking to read the plans of God in these four brief chapters. From grief to greatness, from despair to delight, that is the relocation that God brought to Naomi and Ruth. God transformed their misery into joy, their mourning into dancing (Psalm 30:11).

The story of Naomi and Ruth tells of the miracle of God's faithfulness. These women were alone, with nothing and no one left to care for them. Their lives and their future had never looked so bleak, but they clung to one another and as Ruth vows: 'I will live with you, I will worship by your side. Nothing will separate us but death.' As God does with every word we speak, He heard Ruth's oath, and started to weave His blessing into their lives. In no time at all, they moved from heartache to happiness.

In the same way, we never know where our life's journey will take us. We may hope for prosperity but find poverty; we may leave full, but return empty, but this doesn't mean that our heavenly Father has abandoned us. Forever, He is working behind the scenes to make the best out of the tattered ribbons of our lives [Romans 8:28]. We may have nothing, but with Him it is everything. As we remain steadfast even in the face of unspeakable tragedies, we discover the faithfulness of God to deliver us from darkness to light [John 8:12]. He redeems our lives as we prostrate ourselves at His feet, humbly seeking His provision and protection. Immediately, He covers us and purchases us with His life. What more can we ever ask for? Truly our Redeemer lives!

The Miracle of Motherhood

It's easy to imagine that being able to bear a child is simply a biological fact for women, but as our stories today attest that's simply not the case. Motherhood is never guaranteed and often comes at a great price. It seems God was hinting at that when He spoke to Adam and Eve after their failed obedience in the Garden of Eden, informing Eve of the pain of her labor [Genesis 3: 16]. This would be followed by the even greater heartache when her oldest son killed her second born [Genesis 4]. Whoever said motherhood isn't for cowards, recognized the courage it takes to endure it.

Biology and nurturance aside, the opportunity to conceive and deliver a child is nothing short of a miracle. When I became pregnant with our first child, I came to appreciate the miracle motherhood is. As we weren't planning on having children right away and used the prescribed protection to ensure that it wouldn't happen, imagine our surprise when we discovered within the first six weeks of our marriage that I was with child. It was a pronouncement I had to get my head around. Oh, of course, I wanted children, but I just wasn't imagining it would happen so quickly. When we asked God about this unexpected timing, He explained it this way. At the moment of Jacob's conception, God selected the exact egg to unite with one specific sperm to create the unique combination of DNA strands resulting in this precious child. It was God's intention to create a child with reddish hair like his grandmother, bright blue eyes like his uncle, a quick sharp mind like his grandfather, and the gentle heart of his father. It was God knitting those elements together in my womb as He tenderly explains in Psalm 139: 13,14: *"You made all the delicate, inner parts of my body and knit me together in my mother's womb. Thank you for making me so wonderfully complex! Your workmanship is marvelous—how well I know it."* It's His tender crafting that makes the creation of babies so miraculous.

What are some other things? We can look at the lives of Rebekah, Rachel and Hannah to discover them. In the case of Rebekah, she waited twenty long years before she conceived her twins. What a seeming lifetime of waiting, praying and pleading for children [Genesis 25:19-26]. Yet despite her delight in being with child, Rebekah suffered horribly; so much so, that she asked God why her pregnancy was so difficult. His answer stunned her, setting her family on a collision course with God's will and human intention.

Sadly, Rebekah took God's counsel as a mandate to manipulate events. She bestowed a mother's favor on her younger, heel-grasping son, keeping him close to her side, while allowing her rambunctious eldest son to race about the fields in search of his father's favorite meal. When the boys grew to manhood, and her age-blinded husband Isaac announced his decision to bequeath his blessings on his first-born, Rebekah swung her plan into action: 'Deceive your father and steal your brother's birthright.' Simple instructions, heartbreaking consequences. This betrayal by mother and son completely broke the family apart. It was an arduous twenty-year journey before Jacob made his way back to his father' side, and his mother was already dead, having passed away without ever laying eyes on her beloved son again.

Why do I tell you this seemingly tragic tale? It certainly doesn't suggest that motherhood is miraculous. Oh, but it does if we look around the failures of people and look at the goodness of God. The first thing is that God responded to the earnest prayer of Isaac for his wife to have a child [Genesis 25:21]; He answered, creating not one but two sons with different physical qualities and spiritual destinies. Secondly, God described His purpose for these two boys, explaining to Rebekah her sons' life purpose. This knowledge was provided to bless her. It wasn't to have Rebekah manipulate the situation in order to ensure God's plan reached completion. After all, God doesn't need us to sin – and make no mistake, anger and betrayal is sin – to accomplish His will. Rather it's so we can prayerfully anticipate and participate in what He's doing.

I believe God does want to share with parents the nature and destiny of the children He is creating for them because He wants us to work with Him toward that end. The destiny for Esau and Jacob should have always been a blessing. They had to remember that when they met up twenty years later. Esau was a successful man who'd not suffered in the slightest from losing the birthright or blessing [Genesis 33: 9]. We aren't sure exactly the challenges that he'd faced, but in looking at the trials that Jacob had to overcome, it certainly appeared that Esau's life was easy in comparison. In fact, because Jacob was away from his family for so long there was little evidence that he actually received the financial inheritance and leadership the birthright he stole was meant to supply. In all likelihood, because Esau stayed with his father, he probably led the family in Jacob's absence.

What about Rebekah? Was Rebekah's motherhood a miracle? Absolutely! She was childless for twenty years when God intervened and opened her womb. Perhaps she didn't always make the right parenting choices, but the miracle of her children was nonetheless real, and they were part of God's plan. She, like many mothers must, had to seek God's comfort to soothe the heartache of losing a child due to family conflicts.

Yet the miracle of motherhood continued in the life of her son Jacob and his twelve sons and one daughter. Unfortunately for his wives, Leah and Rachel, they struggled with the miracle of motherhood and children became a battlefield for supremacy in their marriage to Jacob. Their childbearing contest explained in Genesis 29-30 should be a stern warning to anyone who allows the gift of children to become a source of competition and bitterness. That is certainly not what God ever intended as He states in Psalm 127:3: *"Children are a gift from the* LORD; *they are a reward from him."*

Alas in today's many fractured families, children are often seesawed back and forth between the recently separated or divorced couples and the newly formed stepfamilies. Instead of the blessing God designed for a healthy family unit, children are used as bargaining chips to gain the advantage or as pay back for suffering. How can we avoid this? Firstly, we can work to maintain the family, and protect it from outside temptations or influences. If it's too late for that and the damage has already been done, then we can attempt to minimize injury. It's essential that all parties work at keeping the conflicts contained and not force the children to engage in their battles. Yet children can grow through witnessing how their parents resolve damaged relationships and build bridges instead of battering rams.

One of the ways that mothers can do this is by reviewing their children's baby pictures. It helps to rehearse the joy, especially during the years of naughty toddlers, challenging primary schoolers or rebellious teenagers. I look at my children's baby pictures, with their broad smiles and sparkling faces and I remember hugs, and nightly tuck-ins and sweet kisses. Those memories solidify for me the miracle of motherhood.

Hannah certainly understood this [1 Samuel 1]. Although her early years of marriage were filled with the torment as the childless wife of the godly Elkanah, she endured the continuous mockery from Peninnah, her husband's other wife who had succeeded in bearing him multiple children. Peninnah was so vicious in her abuse that Hannah was in tears and sought comfort in the temple where she poured out her misery. Eli, the chief priest, spotted Hannah in her distress and thought she was drunk and disorderly. Thanks to Eli's wicked sons, such behavior was common in the temple. Yet Hannah was not drowning her sorrow but surrendering it to God. When Eli learned of her petitions, he was touched by her humility and offered her his blessings, which sparked hope in Hannah's heart.

Hannah knew God had heard her cry when she gave birth to her first-born son, naming him Samuel, a name which means *"I asked the LORD for him."* [1 Samuel 1:20]. From his first breath, Hannah dedicated him to the Lord, and when he was just a young boy, delivered him to Eli to serve in the temple [1 Samuel 1:27,28]. Of all these women, Hannah truly understood the miracle of motherhood. She knew that her child was a special gift from God, destined to do great things and from an early age dedicated him to this service. It certainly doesn't mean we are to bundle up our little ones and deliver them to our pastor so they can serve in the church. Rather, it's our commitment to train our children in godliness to help them pursue the Lord and devote themselves to His service [Proverbs 22:6].

If we truly recognize the miracle of motherhood, we will surrender our children into the Lord's care. In this way, we allow their nature and training to be directed by the Lord to ensure they fulfill the destiny to which He's called them.

The Miracle of Strength

The story of David and Goliath is one that is told far beyond the pulpit and Sunday school, circling the globe in many creative ways. All of us get excited about the little guy winning over the big monster. It remains the story of legends, inspiring all of us that it's faith and courage, not size that really matters.

It's always worth another look to see how the story is told. The Philistines and the Israelites had long been at war with one another. Their religious beliefs and political and cultural practices were as different as night from day. The Israelites believed that their Creator had selected them as His chosen people, delivered them from 400 years of Egyptian slavery, and hand written His instructions. For centuries He'd given them the leaders they needed who would free them from the marauding tribes that tried to crush or enslave them.

The Philistines were one of the groups who harassed the Israelites. Their Greek name, *palaistinei,* is where we get the word Palestine today and is all that remains of this war-crazed tribe. Descended from Noah's son Ham [Genesis 10], the Philistines had at one time been neighbors of Abraham and Isaac [Genesis 21;26]. However, this alliance frayed when God told the Israelites that the Philistines' land was theirs [Exodus 23]. Yet no matter how often they tried, the Israelites couldn't claim this part of their inheritance, despite God's promises [Joshua 13].

Back and forth went the contest with first one side and then the other achieving significant victories, but it was the Philistines' skill with forging iron weapons that made them a formidable opponent. They even forced Israel to have all their weapons and tools sharpened or repaired by Philistine blacksmiths [1 Samuel 13:19-21], an obligation that was not only humiliating, but imposed a level of submission that destabilized the Israelites in warfare. Yet having superior weaponry was not enough for the battle-hardened Philistines. Always seeking ways to torment the Israelites, the Philistines captured the Ark of the Covenant [1 Samuel 4] in hopes of weakening the Israelites and their relationship with God. However, God used this opportunity to further plague the Philistines, collapsing the statue of their god Dagon not once but twice and releasing horrid boils upon the people, events which forced them to return the Ark [1 Samuel 5].

When the people appointed Saul as King, they hoped he could rally their troops to defeat their enemy. But it was for his careless and continuous disobedience that the kingdom was ripped from Saul and given to the shepherd boy David [1 Samuel 16]. Still the Philistines taunted Israel. Their massive army spread across the fields, shouting curses at the anxious Israelite warriors. If ever there was a time that the Israelites felt like grasshoppers it was then. The Philistine champion Goliath lumbered out on to the field. Standing over nine feet tall, hefting a tree-trunk sized spear in his hand and clothed in bronze armor weighing 125 pounds, Goliath was a behemoth. His mouth was as ugly as his appearance, as he mocked the Israelites' God and king. So confident was he in his battle skills that he offered to personally fight any Israelite opponent [1 Samuel 17:8]. His roar of defiance sent the Israelites into even greater panic. They had no one to compare with Goliath in size or skill amongst their warriors and for the next forty days the Israelites faced the relentless heat of the sun and scorching taunts of their enemy. As each day passed, their situation looked more helpless.

Then innocently Jesse sends his young son David to visit his older brothers on the battlefield. Hoping to hear news of the skirmish and sustain his boys with extra provisions, Jesse calls David from the fields of grazing sheep and sends him to the edge of the battlefield.

David arrived just in time to see Goliath swagger out and deliver his daily taunt. David heard not only Goliath's taunt, but the Israelites' proclamation of a substantial reward. Perhaps it was the exuberance of youth that compelled David to ask about the prize or perhaps he wanted to enrich his father. Given that David generally seemed disinterested in fighting for payment throughout his career, it may have been the latter. Whatever the case, his oldest brother Eliab heard David's questions and rebuked him for it, but David was not dissuaded and persisted until finally he stood before the King. Saul studied the youth, recognizing a ruddy, handsome young man who was not a warrior, but a farmer. *"Don't be ridiculous!" Saul replied. "There's no way you can fight this Philistine and possibly win! You're only a boy, and he's been a man of war since his youth."* [1 Samuel 17:33]

It was then that David stated his unlikely warrior credentials: *"I have been taking care of my father's sheep and goats," he said. "When a lion or a bear comes to steal a lamb from the flock, I go after it with a club and rescue the lamb from its mouth. If the animal turns on me, I catch it by the jaw and club it to death. I have done this to both lions and bears, and I'll do it to this pagan Philistine, too, for he has defied the armies of the living God! The LORD who rescued me from the claws of the lion and the bear will rescue me from this Philistine!"* [1 Samuel 17:34-37]

Saul, impressed by the fiery passion and courageous heart of this youth, finally consented. At first Saul tried to suit up David with his own heavy armor, but the uncomfortable weight made movement almost impossible. It was then that David selected the only weapons that he needed, a shepherd's weapons, five smooth stones, tucking them securely into his shepherd's bag. Then wearing only his shepherd's smock and bag, he strode out onto the battlefield. A hush settled over the hillside for this was the first time that anyone from the Israelite army had stepped out to fight. Then laughter rippled through the Philistine warriors. 'A boy, they've sent a boy,' they sneered. Goliath roared in rage at the insult: *"Am I a dog,"* he roared at David, *"that you come at me with a stick?"* And he cursed David by the names of his gods. *"Come over here, and I'll give your flesh to the birds and wild animals!" Goliath yelled."* [1 Samuel 17:43-44]

Undaunted by the mammoth size of the enemy or his ugly jeers, David stepped forward. His response were the words of legends: *"You come to me with sword, spear, and javelin, but I come to you in the name of the LORD of Heaven's Armies—the God of the armies of Israel, whom you have defied. Today the LORD will conquer you"*... *"This is the LORD's battle, and he will give you to us!"* [1 Samuel 17:45-47]

So confident was David that when Goliath lumbered closer to pluck out his heart, David, without hesitation, raced forward to meet him. As he sprinted, he pulled out a single stone from his bag and placed it into his sling. Whipping it over his shoulder, he aimed it, not for the massive body which would be a perfect and easy target, but for his forehead where it would do the most damage. And his aim was true, striking the Philistine with such force, that it made a huge dent in Goliath's skull. Stumbling from the impact of the blow, Goliath crashed to the ground unconscious. To finish the job, David hefted Goliath's own sword and sliced off his enemy's head.

You can imagine the stunned silence on both sides of the field. For a few seconds nothing was heard, but then the Philistines, recognizing that their champion was dead and recognizing that slavery or death awaited them, turned and made a mad dash from the field. Hot on their heels they heard the triumphant war cry of the Israelites. It was a victory almost as memorable as the parting of the Red Sea. And in both instances God was there.

Did you notice that David selected the elements of God's earth and not the armor and weapons made of human hands? Every part of this victory can be attributed directly to God, and David himself was the first to say it: *"Everyone assembled here will know that the Lord rescues His people, but not with sword and spear."* [1 Samuel 17:47]. He repeats this in Psalm 20:7: *"Some nations boast of their chariots and horses, but we boast in the name of the Lord our God."*

It was echoed again when centuries later King Jehoshaphat faced an equally overwhelming army [2 Chronicles 20:15], and the prophet Zechariah [4:6] encouraged Zerubbabel with similar words: *"It is not by force nor by strength, but by my Spirit, says the Lord of Heaven's Armies."* Even the writer of Proverbs [21:31] understood that it's God who wins the hopeless battles: *"The horse is prepared for the day of battle, but the victory belongs to the Lord."*

So it is with us. We do not gain the victory over our enemy by the size of our bank account or the wealth of our knowledge, or position of our friends or weight of our family's legacy. We gain the victory by the hand of the Lord. He is the one that gives us the best battle strategies and – even if it is a single smooth stone – the enemy will fall just as soundly, never to rise again.

Praise be the Lord. That is the miracle of His strength.

Courage in the Flames

The fiery furnace is a story that thrills us every time we hear it. Three young Jewish boys, captured in their homeland and dragged across the country, find themselves in King Nebuchadnezzar's court. They had watched as the Babylonian army attacked their city, home and family. Then they were forced to trudge nearly 900 miles, a journey taking approximately four months before reaching their enemy's royal city. They'd even watched as the weaker amongst them were culled from the group so that "*only strong, healthy and good-looking young men*" [Daniel 1:4] were selected for special training. The king himself ordered Ashpenaz, his chief of staff to train them with the necessary skills, even allocating rich foods from his own kitchen to nourish them. For three years they underwent this rigorous education, similar to a university bachelor's degree today, and only after successfully graduating from their study did they enter the royal service.

Four of these young men: Daniel, Hananiah, Mishael and Azariah, surrendered their Jewish names and adopted the requisite Babylonian titles: Belteshazzar, Shadrach, Meshach and Abednego. Yet they refused to defile themselves with the irreligious food offered them. They knew and practiced the Mosaic law and would not put in their mouths food that did not adhere to those requirements. Normally Ashpenaz would ignore the requests of his charges, especially for their religious reasons, practices foreign to him, and therefore of little consequence, but there was something about Daniel and his friends. He could see their wisdom, strength and humility and knew that they would excel at their training, yet he feared his king, a man always acting on the edge of madness. Any failure could be fatal, and thus he warned them: *"If you become pale and thin compared to the other youths your age, I am afraid the king will have me beheaded."* [Daniel 1:10] Daniel appreciated the dilemma so negotiated: *"Please test us for ten days on a diet of vegetables and water." "At the end of the ten days, see how we look compared to the other young men who are eating the king's food. Then make your decision in light of what you see."* [Daniel 1:12,13] The results were spectacular and conclusive and the young men *"looked healthier and better nourished than the young men who had been eating the food assigned by the king."* [Daniel 1:15]

But it wasn't just their physical appearance that set them apart; they were head and shoulders above everyone else in their studies. Not only that, God had blessed Daniel with the special ability to interpret visions and dreams. At graduation, when the king interviewed the students, no one compared to these young men and *"he found them ten times more capable than any of the magicians and enchanters in his entire kingdom."* [Daniel 1:20]

He then made his assignments: Shadrach, Meshach and Abednego were given charge of all the affairs in the Babylonian province, but he kept Daniel in his own court as one of his personal advisors, a role Daniel would have throughout the reign of four kings. Yet despite their authority and responsibility, these men were always under scrutiny and others were jealous of their positions, and angry that foreign captives were afforded such elevated positions. These men looked to make trouble, and it wasn't long brewing.

As his madness and god-complex swelled, King Nebuchadnezzar ordered a massive, ninety-foot golden statue be erected and when the music played, everyone was to bow in homage to it. Disobedience meant instant death. When the moment came, everyone bent their knee. Only three men remained standing straight and tall above the crowd: Shadrach, Meshach and Abednego. This delighted their jealous enemies, who dashed off to tattle to the king. The unstable king flew into a rage and gave them one more chance to worship his idol. He couldn't believe anyone would be that foolish to defy him, but there they stood, their stance and answer resolute: *"If we are thrown into the blazing furnace, the God whom we serve is able to save us. He will rescue us from your power, Your Majesty. But even if he doesn't, we want to make it clear to you, Your Majesty, that we will never serve your gods or worship the gold statue you have set up."* [Daniel 3:17,18]

Sputtering with rage, Nebuchadnezzar demanded the furnace be stoked to its hottest level. He even ordered his soldiers to bind the dissidents before tossing them into the flames. The temperature was so hot, the soldiers collapsed from the heat, before heaving Shadrach, Meshach and Abednego into the furnace. To everyone's amazement, the men stood, dusted themselves off, and took a stroll in the oven with a fourth figure, who, like them, remained untouched by the fire, his ethereal glow even brighter than the flames. This was beyond anything that Nebuchadnezzar had ever witnessed for the fourth looked like a supernatural being. Calling them out of the flames, the king discovered an even a further miracle. Not only had they survived the scorching heat, but *"Not a hair on their heads was singed, and their clothing was not scorched. They didn't even smell of smoke."* [Daniel 3:27]

The king didn't need his magicians to tell him what had happened. This was a miracle, and he declared it so: *"Praise to the God of Shadrach, Meshach, and Abednego! He sent his angel to rescue his servants who trusted in him. They defied the king's command and were willing to die rather than serve or worship any god except their own God."* [Daniel 3:28] This crazed king filled with an unquenchable lust for power and glory could not deny what he'd witnessed. Nothing he could do or build would match the power he'd just witnessed. No God was greater than the One who'd performed the unimaginable and rescued these men.

Their act of obedience transformed a king and his kingdom. God's name was praised, and Shadrach, Meshach and Abednego were promoted to even higher positions for their godly dedication. But that isn't the purpose of this story: personal elevation and glory. It's meaningless in the scheme of things. What's important is their dedication in the face of death, standing for God instead of bowing to the enemy. That's what we remember here. The writer of Hebrews tells us about those who were called to do the same, who by faith: *"quenched the flames of fire, and escaped death by the edge of the sword. Their weakness was turned to strength. They became strong in battle and put whole armies to flight."* [Hebrews 11:34]

And we never know when we'll be called to do the same. When we'll be called to have the courage of Shadrach, Meshach and Abednego, three youths who for their love of God faced the fiery furnace, walked through the flames, and stepped out unscathed. Will our faith be tested? Absolutely! Every day! Will our God be with us? Resoundingly Yes! In any flames or through any fire, He walks with us, by our side offering His strength to see us through. Shadrach, Meshach and Abednego believed – so can we.

Facing the Lions

God prevails again in the unforgettable story of Daniel. A man gifted with God's wisdom, he'd lived a life of faithfulness through the madness of King Nebuchadnezzar and the licentiousness of King Belshazzar. Now he was serving Darius the Mede, a ruler who, like the others before him, noted Daniel's administrative genius. Consistently Daniel outshone all the other counselors and because of his excellence, Darius was getting ready to appoint him as his chief of staff. The thought of a foreigner taking on such a coveted role enraged the other officials and they determined to discredit Daniel, yet they knew him to be faultless in his governance. There was only one area in which he was vulnerable – his faith. They would catch him here, they thought. Thus, they tricked Darius into signing a law forbidding worship of any other god but him [Daniel 6:6-9]. Daniel wasn't perturbed by this news. He'd lived through too much to be worried by such a law. He'd seen God do too many incredible things to surrender his habit of worship, and so he openly continued to pray daily, to the malicious delight of his enemies who eagerly ran to the king with their tale: 'Daniel continues to pray to his god, not you. He's defying your order. You must kill him.'

Darius was distressed at this news. He knew this charge was the result of petty jealousies even as he knew that Daniel was the best of men. Desperately, he tried to save him, but couldn't find a loop hole in his decree. Reluctantly he sent his soldiers and, with his own prayer told Daniel: *"May your God, whom you serve so faithfully, rescue you"* [Daniel 6:16] before sealing Daniel into the lions' den. Darius spent a sleepless night, hoping, praying, his advisor would be spared. At the crack of dawn, he rushed to the mouth of the den, shouting: *"Daniel, servant of the living God! Was your God, whom you serve so faithfully, able to rescue you from the lions?"* [Daniel 6:20] Imagine his immense relief when he heard Daniel's strong, clear voice: *"Long live the king! My God sent his angel to shut the lions' mouths so that they would not hurt me, for I have been found innocent in his sight. And I have not wronged you, Your Majesty."* [Daniel 6:21]

Like so many before him, Daniel wasn't alone in his darkest hour. He may have heard the growls of ravenous lions, but he also heard the calming voice of God's messenger, soothing these wild beasts. Nothing can withstand the Lion of Judah and His creation will always be subdued before Him. Daniel discovered this in his prison as his friends Shadrach, Meshach and Abednego discovered it in their furnace. Wherever we are, God is [Psalm 139:7-12].

How did Darius feel when he heard his friend still lived? He was ecstatic and immediately pulled Daniel from the pit. After a frantic search to ensure Daniel's safety, he discovered there wasn't a bite or claw mark anywhere on his body. Darius may have been helpless to intervene, but God wasn't constrained by natural or political laws. He commanded and the lions' jaws were sealed shut and He continues to seal the devil's mouth from devouring His people [1 Peter 5:8]. Only the God of the Universe could do that. Armed with this knowledge, Darius issued a new decree, commanding *"that everyone throughout my kingdom should tremble with fear before the God of Daniel. For he is the living God, and he will endure forever. His kingdom will never be destroyed, and his rule will never end. He rescues and saves his people; he performs miraculous signs and wonders in the heavens and on earth. He has rescued Daniel from the power of the lions."* [Daniel 6:26,27] Once again God miraculously rescued one of His children, not only saving his life from certain death, but ensuring that the entire region would hear of God's greatness and power.

Let our lives be a testimony of God's greatness. Let others witness His miraculous power as we stand firm in Him. May our faith, whether the size of a mustard seed or a mighty oak, illustrate His mercy and willingness to save that His name may be praised through the earth.

The Miracle of the Message

Our final story involves Jonah, a young prophet from Gath-hepher, an area near Nazareth in the northern region of Israel. Jeroboam II was king, a defiant, worldly ruler who built pagan shrines and installed unauthorized priests. The prophet Amos had been commissioned to speak against his wickedness, and undoubtedly Jonah hoped for a similar commission, but God had other plans, directing him to Nineveh instead [Jonah 1:2]. Jonah was hailed as a prophet [2 Kings 14:25] who spoke for God, yet in our story, it seems that Jonah had lost his focus.

When God called him, instead of leaping up and rushing to obey, Jonah headed in the exact opposite direction, racing to one of the most distant destinations possible. Fleeing Nazareth, Jonah raced the sixty miles to Joppa, a port city on the Mediterranean Sea. There he jumped onto a ship heading to Tarshish. Not only would it take him as far away as possible from Nineveh, but the mode of transportation he chose was the fastest possible. Obedience would have required an eastward journey of 500 miles by land, but instead he chose a water route taking him 2,500 miles west. He was determined to avoid God's call and wanted nothing to do with the Assyrians and their potential redemption.

Why did he hate the Assyrians so much? For centuries, they'd been a thorn in the side of the Israelites. Moreover, they were beyond evil in their worship and ruthless when conquering other nations. Jonah had no desire to see these hated people repent from their innumerable sins. In Jonah's mind, they deserved destruction and he wanted to see them suffer for their brutality. Yet God, in His mercy, had other plans and wanted Jonah to participate in them. He could have chosen another messenger, but He didn't. He wanted His prophet Jonah to be the one to accomplish this project, perhaps to transform the prejudice and hatred in Jonah's heart.

What then did God do? He sent a violent tempest that threatened to tear the ship apart [Jonah 1]. Oblivious to the pounding waves and slashing winds, Jonah slept peacefully, and the sailors had to shake him awake. In a desperate effort to avert catastrophe, lots were cast to see who'd angered God. Jonah confessed his culpability and advised they throw him into the sea. Strangely, Jonah preferred disobedience and death to heeding God's call. Thus, the sailors reluctantly tossed him overboard and the roaring winds and mountainous waves consumed him. As the storm receded to a whisper, the sailors observed a huge fish leap out of the diminishing waves and swallow the errant prophet whole, before it splashed back into the water. As far as the sailors were concerned, Jonah had paid for his defiance.

But this is only the beginning of the story. This God-ordained aquatic was specifically created and commissioned to consume Jonah in one gulp. Moreover, the fish was made in such a fashion to ensure that his acidic stomach gasses wouldn't destroy Jonah. God needed him in this quiet place to give the recalcitrant messenger an opportunity to repent. Although some may doubt the veracity of this story as being too impossible to imagine, we who believe Scripture to be the infallible Word of God do not question its possibility. As it is with every miracle recorded in the Bible, we either accept the impossible and believe in the amazing, or we deny it all: the Virgin Birth, Daniel and his lions, Shadrach, Meshach and Abednego and the flames, Moses and the Red Sea, and Christ's resurrection. With the Bible, it's always an all or nothing decision as we can't cut and paste what we choose to believe and what we don't. I choose to believe it all.

So where does that leave us with Jonah: sloshing about in the belly of a huge fish. The unpleasantness of the experience brought Jonah to his knees, and he prayed in earnest [Jonah 2]. At last he was willing to complete the task God set for him, but it took the belly of a fish to bring him to his knees. Finally, he headed to Nineveh and shouted to the crowds that destruction was coming. There was no love and forgiveness in his message; after all Jonah had none for these rebellious people. It was harsh words of judgement. Yet, amazingly, the people listened and repented. Even the king abandoned his royal robes for coarse burlap and covered himself in ashes. His repentance was genuine, and he urged everyone to *"turn from their evil ways and stop all their violence. Who can tell? Perhaps even yet God will change his mind and hold back his fierce anger from destroying us."* [Jonah 3:8,9]

God was touched by their sincere contrition. Instead of judgement, He showed mercy. This should have been a moment of triumph for Jonah. He was sent to bring a message, albeit a difficult one, and he witnessed an entire city turn from evil and to God. What a victory! But the book of Jonah doesn't end at chapter 3; we still have another chapter and here we read that Jonah was livid that God didn't destroy the Ninevites. He moaned: *"Didn't I say before I left home that you would do this, Lord? That is why I ran away to Tarshish! I knew that you are a merciful and compassionate God, slow to get angry and filled with unfailing love. You are eager to turn back from destroying people. Just kill me now, Lord! I'd rather be dead than alive if what I predicted will not happen."* [Jonah 4:2,3]

His reaction shocks us, doesn't it? What, we may ask? You don't like that God is merciful and compassionate. You don't want God to be slow to anger and filled with unfailing love. How is that possible? Clearly Jonah's hatred for the Ninevites was deeper and more pervasive than his compassion and forgiveness. Still God doesn't give up on Jonah, hoping he, too, will repent. Yet Jonah pouted instead and ran to the far side of the city – not as far as he ran the first time, because likely he still hoped to see God's judgement.

Thus, he watched and waited in the hot sun for days on end, hoping against hope that God would send His fiery destruction on this wicked city. But nothing happened. The people remained repentant and God remained compassionate just as did for his stubborn messenger. He sprouted a plant to shield Jonah from the fierce sun's heat. But Jonah's bitterness grew, and so God sent a worm to nibble away at the tender roots of the plant, destroying Jonah's undeserved shade. Then He turned up the heat with a scorching east wind. Once more Jonah grouched: *"Death is certainly better than living like this!"* [Jonah 4:8].

God tried to get through to him: *"Is it right for you to be angry because the plant died?"* Jonah thought his whining justified. First the call, then the whale, next the repentant people, and now the withered plant. 'Life wasn't worth living,' moaned Jonah. Then the LORD made His point: *"You feel sorry about the plant, though you did nothing to put it there. It came quickly and died quickly. But Nineveh has more than 120,000 people living in spiritual darkness, not to mention all the animals. Shouldn't I feel sorry for such a great city?"* [Jonah 4:10,11]

'Where is your priorities Jonah,' God was asking. 'Are you concerned for souls or your own reputation? Do you seek mercy or justice? Will you let your bitterness win out over My redemption?' God wanted Jonah to learn a lesson both about His character and his own for God's desire is that no one will perish [2 Peter 3:9].

And on that profound note the story ends. In just four chapters and forty verses God succinctly explains His mission objective. No matter how wicked or evil, God desires that all come to the saving knowledge of His Son Jesus Christ. Thus, we are instructed to *"Go into all the world and preach the Good News to everyone"* [Mark 16:15] because He has made us a light in order to bring salvation to everyone on earth [Acts 13:47]. Even to the unlovely – for they are loved by God. We can be part of this miracle by sharing His love with others. Let's not run from that call but reach for it and embrace it every day.

Conclusion

This devotional hasn't exhausted all the miraculous events in the Bible. There are still many others that can be explored. Perhaps you'd like to write about them and search the Scriptures to read about them. What's important is to see how God personally impacts the lives of His people, steps into their reality to create a new one. That's how loving and intimate our Savior is. He hears our prayers, knows our needs and responds in ways we can't even imagine.

I hope this text re-invigorates your faith for the impossible. In our complex world, God is never out of His depth, confused as to how to make the wrong, right, or uncertain about what to do in any given situation. What a relief to know that He is still the Creator of the Universe and can alter any scientific reality to show His children His enormous love and immeasurable power. He is always confident, completely effective and continuously operating in the amazing.

I would recommend that you return to the Word to read these miracles once again. Keep a record of your own miracles or others that you've heard. Be encouraged by what God has done for you and others. Record and recount them so that when life seems overwhelming, you'll remember that there is a God who cares and is able to do the impossible. Hold fast to the truth that God sees, knows and can do all things.

I have designed a sample sheet on which you can record your miracles. Make copies of it if you'd like, or design your own. God wants us to collect memories, like Joshua's memorial stones, to remember what He's done for us. Then despite the season, whether sun-filled or rain-drenched, we can recall how He miraculously intervened on our behalf to save, to heal, to direct, or to rescue that we may live in His grace and others may see His glory.

Every blessing on your journey. See you in Heaven.

In His Grace,

Dianne

A Miraculous Life

Event:

_____

Date:

_____

People Involved:

_____
_____
_____
_____

Description:

_____
_____
_____
_____
_____
_____
_____

Prayer:

_____
_____
_____
_____